WHAT'S YOURS IS MINE

When a REALIST Marries an Idealist

STACY WILLOUGHBY

Wishing you
and your
honey lots
of love and money!

Stacy Willoughby

Copyright © 2012 Stacy Willoughby

This book is designed to provide information on the subject of personal finance. As each individual situation is unique, questions relevant to personal finances and specific to the individual should be addressed to an appropriate professional to ensure that the situation has been evaluated carefully and appropriately. The au-thor and publisher specifically disclaim any liability, loss, or risk which is incurred as a consequence, directly or indirectly, of the use and publication of any of the contents of this work.

Stacy Willoughby
www.StacyWilloughby.com

Sunday Brunch Books
PMB #136
4320 196th Street S.W. #B
Lynnwood, WA 98036

ISBN: 978-0-9859176-0-9
Library of Congress Control Number: 2001012345

Cover design by Tracy Niemczal
Interior text layout by Gorham Printing

Printed in the United States by Gorham Printing
www.gorhamprinting.com

CONTENTS

To Rick, who is making all my dreams come true.

INTRODUCTION

Being a romantic at heart and an eternal optimist, I believe that everything is possible. When you and your spouse bring the best of yourselves to your marriage, the victories you can achieve are powerful. Knowing that you have this person in your life that you trust completely and receive unfailing support from, and who knows the secret dreams of your heart, is a potent feeling.

Still, in today's world, maintaining a strong relationship in which money doesn't get in the way can be hard. The decade began with the tech bubble burst in 2001 and ended with the Great Recession. With the results of this last decade and changes in our personal economies, we are more aware of our finances than we were in the past. We now publicly talk about this subject, which once was taboo. But for couples these discussions can be thorny, especially if the family's breadwinner loses a job, if one or both earners in a two-income household find themselves underemployed, or if a formerly passive partner starts to take a more active role in financial decision making. Inequities in earnings or spending can contribute to fights, resentment, and conflict.

Traditionally, financial roles were well defined for men and women. Today, both men and women fill a variety of financial roles, so it can be hard to know the standards for maintaining a strong relationship in which money doesn't get in the way of happiness. Reverting to traditional roles isn't the answer. Keeping an open mind, compromising, and communicating will help.

Other factors can make talking about money feel like walking into a minefield. I believe that because we are not taught about money and personal finance at school, we acquire our financial habits and beliefs from our experiences. Those experiences forge our emotional attachments to money, making financial conversations with a partner difficult. You may feel inadequate, immature, or inexperienced when handling money or, alternatively, use it to exert control or power. You may fall into old patterns established by your parents or previous loves. These behaviors can sabotage the best intentions for your relationship.

The goal of this book is to help you and your spouse understand that you are not alone in your issues with money. Throughout the book, I delve into the experiences and conversations I shared with Rick, my husband, so you can see how natural it is to get tripped up by financial issues. When we ran into a new problem, we knew many of the right things to do, but understanding how to do them together as a married couple was a hurdle. We have learned from what we have done right and, more important, from what we got completely wrong. Our secret is to try to be tender and, out of love and respect for each other and our relationship, not to hurt one another.

Overall, in our relationship, Rick is the realist and I am the idealist. I dream up the big idea, and he slows me down to figure out if the time is right for that big idea. However, neither of us fits those labels all the time. On occasion, he has decided to take a risk that I had to think about twice or three times. As a general rule, I don't like labels. If one of you in the relationship bears the label of "spender" or "saver," that becomes the default explanation for behavior. I prefer understanding the reasons for each decision to spend or save. Both of you could learn by having conversations and by delving deeper.

I don't have all the answers to the financial problems you might face, but by reading these real-life stories, you might find the tools and courage to have candid conversations with your partner. In this book, I encourage you both to engage in periodic conversations to explore your experiences and emotions. Having these conversations during a time when the outcome isn't immediately relevant is helpful. You could have these talks without pressure during a long drive or a walk around the neighborhood, for example. To support talking on a regular, scheduled basis, try a Sunday brunch. On a Sunday morning, assemble your brunch, get cozy in your breakfast nook, and enjoy a mimosa with your eggs and bacon. During your meal, you can say, "I was just reading about this couple, and they had an issue with talking about money, just like us." Then open up this book to the Sunday brunch conversation that you want to engage in and see what unfolds. I have also included tips on getting organized. Look for these when you are trying to tackle the nuts and bolts of a particular issue, like paying off debt or buying a home.

Through my work, I hear of various experiences similar to those I shared with Rick. So in this book, I hope to inspire you to reach for your dreams as well as those of your spouse. I want you to feel empowered to have those difficult financial conversations with your partner.

As you approach each challenge, remember that having more money isn't the simple solution that it may seem to be. You have probably heard stories of lottery winners whose marriages and family relationships were damaged after a large win. I believe that love is a stronger base for building the foundation of your financial plan.

In fact, love is the reason that I write this book. Love gives me the courage to share this story. Love is the reason to go all out and let go of fear. Living on love can help a family transcend its daily struggles. No names have been changed in this book. The stories are real, sometimes funny, and sometimes painful. I invite you to share your story too.

1

FULL DISCLOSURE

On yet another rainy, lazy Sunday morning in Seattle, I was snuggling in bed with my husband. I said to him that I didn't think anyone in the world could possibly be as in love as we were at that moment. He responded, "I hope not." This perplexed me, and I asked, "What does that mean?" He explained, "I sure hope that millions more get to feel as in love as we are right now." Insight like that makes me fall in love with him all over again.

Rick and I first met at work. We were both involved in setting up a new retail store when I noticed him. Rick, a finish carpenter, was building the interior. I was a department manager excited to help establish a flagship store. In the weeks before the store opening, we got to know each other a little. He liked to joke around, and I liked the way his eyes smiled. Once, he fixed my hard hat, explaining that it should stay put, perched above my head, and not fall down into my eyes.

A week after the store's grand opening, Rick stopped by my department to see how things were going. He wore a sport coat and tie, which surprised me. I was used to seeing him in a T-shirt and jeans, both covered with sawdust. We chatted for a few minutes and then said goodbye. I still didn't know him that well outside of work.

Later that afternoon, while I was at work, Rick called and asked me to dinner. Luckily for both of us, I said yes. I was a little nervous about going on that date. After breaking up with my fiancé a couple of years before, I had sworn off men. But something about Rick prompted me to go out with him. I was curious about who he was. I was ready to start dating again. He seemed so different from the guys I used to date.

For dinner, he introduced me to a wonderful family-owned Italian restaurant. I was completely surprised by what a great time I had. We made conversation easily, learning so much more about each other. We were both Navy brats, and our fathers had both retired from the military. Rick was thirty-eight years old to my twenty-five years, and he had a son who was twelve. At the end of that evening on November 23, 1999, I was already looking forward to the next time we would see each other.

We dated for a while, and I became completely smitten. I thought about Rick constantly. Neither one of us is known for wanting to spend a lot of time on the phone, but we did. Rick shared custody of his son, Matt, with his ex-wife. Until Rick was ready to introduce us, I stayed away on the days when Matt was over. When Matt was at his mom's house, Rick and I spent a lot of time together.

A couple of months into our relationship, we decided to go away for the weekend. We drove to Cannon Beach, a great spot on the Oregon coast. We spent our time holding hands, exploring the town, walking the beach, and hanging out at the local restaurants. Rick is six feet one to my four feet eight, so on the beach when we approached a piece of driftwood, I would stand on it so he didn't have to lean down so far to kiss me. This became a game of ours.

We had a room at a cute little lodge with a large picture window overlooking the ocean. One evening, a big storm rolled in, and we stayed inside to watch the wind, the waves, and the lightning. A gas fireplace and a bottle of champagne made us cozy. Nestled by the fire with a blanket and Rick's arm around me felt like the exact place that I was supposed to be. The storm knocked out the power, but we didn't notice until much later. We were too engrossed in the storm and in each other. I still tell my friends that it was during this weekend that I fell in love with Rick.

I have heard that when you are in love, your brain produces chemicals that encourage the euphoric feeling people know as love. Scientists say these chemicals produce an effect very much like a drug high. It's easy to understand why all rational and logical thought leave your mind when these chemicals are released. You want to see the best in the other person and also want that person to see only the best in you. You might gloss over ugly details of your partner's past relationships or paint a rosier financial picture. You might overlook faults and habits that you normally find irritating.

With time, the euphoric feeling gradually wears off, and you start to dig into the nitty-gritty details about each other. You probably meet each other's parents. You spend time in your respective homes. You see the inside of your partner's medicine cabinet. You find out whether this person prefers Miracle Whip or mayonnaise. You hear about many of the events that helped shape the object of your affection.

Eventually, you begin to see your partner in your future. Imagining life without that person becomes harder and harder.

And so you muster the courage to begin that difficult conversation: the Money Talk. Or maybe your partner brings it up, catching you off guard. Together, you acknowledge that you haven't had this conversation before, but want to share and get a better understanding of each other's finances. You set aside a time in the future that you can devote to the conversation.

COMING CLEAN

Having the Money Talk involves asking about each other's financial situation and trying not to judge. This is the moment when you are both supposed to lay it all out on the table. Assets, income, debt, cash flow, and net worth are up for discussion (see glossary on page 157). These may sound more like terms for evaluating a business, but they are important to know when you start taking the next steps as a couple.

At this point, it isn't important how big or small the numbers are. What's key is full disclosure. Having the Money Talk doesn't mean that you have to share a checkbook, credit cards, or financial advisor. Those are separate decisions that are based on where you are in your relationship and where you are headed.

Each of us has been raised differently and has distinct ways of dealing with money. Even siblings reared by the same parents will have varying approaches. Use the Money Talk to get basic information about your partner's personality around money. Does that person tend to spend or save more? How does that fit with your money personality? What financial views do you share in common? What are your differences? What is the source of those differences? When you talk about finances, is your partner interested, condescending, or nonchalant? Do you have hang-ups about money that have not surfaced until now? What are your dreams or aspirations for the future? What are your partner's dreams? What impact could your partner's financial situation have on your aspirations?

Next, try to understand more-specific information. Who and what else could become the financial responsibility of one or both of you? For example, are you supporting children from a former spouse? At this time, you might further discuss assets and liabilities, income and debt. This conversation can be very emotionally draining, so consider tackling it in chunks over a few weeks, as Rick and I did.

Having this talk can be scary, embarrassing, cumbersome, or awkward. As a society, we don't talk honestly about our personal finances in public. Like many, I was taught that speaking about money is bad etiquette. But coming clean about finances is critical to moving forward in your relationship together. Keep this thought in mind: You have already decided to share your heart with this person; why is it so hard to share your financial situation? I don't believe that people value money over love. I think we are self-conscious about our financial status and fear that we will be judged inadequate or loved only for our money.

Fear of the outcome may also make us afraid to have the Money Talk. What if you find out that your partner is a compulsive spender, a hoarder, or a gambler? What if he or she has bad credit because of a recent messy divorce, but has a plan to repair the credit rating? What if your partner now knows what you have been trying to hide? What if he or she isn't receptive to having the conversation and has difficulty participating? What if information uncovered by the Money Talk makes both of you unsure that you want to continue as a couple? That is always a possibility, especially before you are married. Fortunately, a lot of resources and people who care about you are available to help.

You can go to your parents, friends, therapists, financial advisors, and others for financial counsel. They can help you navigate this unfamiliar territory. That first honest and frank discussion about money is probably the hardest. The good news is that talking about money does get easier the longer you are together. Some of the principles that help create a good conversation the first time can also help you later in your relationship.

MAKING INROADS

Rick and I didn't have the full conversation about money until we had been together for a year and a half. Before that, we knew a lot about the general health of each other's finances, but not the details. I had my own condo, which I'd bought months before I started seeing him. But then my roommate decided to move closer to work, and I had to make a decision: find a new roommate, rent out my condo, or sell it. At this point in my relationship with Rick, I wanted to move in with him, but I wasn't sure if that was even an option.

This situation prompted our Money Talk. Rick did not feel ready to have the conversation, but he was willing to try so we could figure out whether I should move in with him and whether I should rent or sell my condo. First I shared a few events that influenced why I deal with money the way I do. I relayed anecdotes that illustrated my money personality. Then I laid it all out for him: my income, how much I paid for the condo, my mortgage balance and payment, and my credit card debt and car payment. This enabled him to understand where I was financially and helped him feel more comfortable sharing his own financial situation with me. Finally, I proposed that I move in with Rick and rent out the condo, and I asked him to lend his carpentry skills toward upgrading it for a tenant.

When it was time for Rick to talk, he had a hard time expanding on his ideas about finances. For the most part, he uses three words to say what I would in twenty. He had his way of doing things, and that was what worked for him. But through open-ended questions and a lot of patience, I was able to glean enough details to make me feel comfortable with his financial foundation. Now I understood his financial obligations for his son. I learned that essentially he was a saver, but that he had no experience investing. In general, he was comfortably living within his means and felt prepared financially in the event of an emergency.

After discussing our individual finances, Rick agreed to the plan I had proposed. I moved in with him and rented out my condo. While I lived at Rick's house, our respective financial situations didn't change much. I paid him rent; we kept our separate bank accounts and didn't pry into each other's choices about money. The difference was that we understood each other's financial situations and felt comfortable moving forward.

AFTER THE TALK

Once you have the conversation, or in our case conversations, what do you do with the information? The point isn't to judge what is right or wrong, because there are many right ways to manage finances. The goal is to see if your partner's approach will work well with yours—that is, to determine if you can achieve compatibility and workability. Are there overlaps, or areas where your individual approaches dovetail into each other? Where are the gaps between your situations? Could those gaps lead to miscommunications, fights, or disagreements? Do you have enough common ground to work around those gaps?

Ultimately, you choose whether your partner and his or her financial situation is a good fit. Making an informed choice about compatibility in money styles is an important factor for your future. Rick and I joke that we are a good match because we both prefer Miracle Whip to mayonnaise, but that is not enough to build a relationship on. Love, compatibility, and communication are fundamental. Communicating well about finances can even help overcome the gap between different money styles.

Fortunately, you have time to figure out if you have common ground to build on from a financial perspective. And you will need time to process the information you receive and your observations. Even after you have had the Money Talk, inconsistencies will arise. I used to tease Rick about his inconsistent behavior. For instance, he told me that he had a hard time spending money on himself. Yet one evening I noticed a new set of tall, black speakers in his family room. I joked that he obviously did not find it difficult to spend money on himself. He said that he bought them because I thought his old speakers were ugly. Years later, I still don't believe that he bought those speakers to please my aesthetic sensibilities.

Over time, your partner's opinions and priorities regarding money may change. Yours might, too. The manner in which you both manage your finances will evolve. You may need to renegotiate financial roles and responsibilities. Those are natural reactions to life changes, lessons learned about money, your partner, and your relationship. Those ongoing changes mean that regular conversations with your partner are even more important, not just at the beginning of your relationship, but throughout it.

GETTING ORGANIZED

....

TIPS FOR THE MONEY TALK

- Inform your partner that you want to have the talk at an agreed upon time in the future.

- Set up a time to talk in a neutral place.

- Keep respect at the front of your mind, and leave judgment aside initially.

- Ensure that you both have information ready about the following (see glossary on page 157):

  o Income and expenses

  o Assets (savings, property, investments)

  o Liabilities (mortgage balance, credit cards, loans)

  o Other obligations (spousal maintenance or alimony, child support, or aid to aging parents)

  o Credit score

  o Dreams

  o Aspirations

2

FOR THE LOVE OF MONEY

Money intrigued me as a child—not just the spending of it, but the process of acquiring and saving it. I had a head for math at an early age and appreciated the practical applications of addition and subtraction. I kept a notebook where, in carefully hand-drawn columns, I would list the money I received on birthdays and Christmas and subtract the purchases I made. You can imagine how I struggled to account for the surprise five-dollar bill I found in the pocket of my winter coat one year.

One of my earliest memories involving money is the day my parents helped my brother and me set up our own savings accounts. I was about five years old, and Loren, my brother, was about three. I clearly remember all four of us sitting on my parents' bed, dumping out the piggy bank, and counting the coins and few bills. We divided the proceeds from our piggy bank into two piles, and Loren and I each deposited about thirty-four dollars into our new savings accounts at my parents' credit union.

From that point forward, we received mailed bank statements

addressed to us personally. Those statements comforted me, given that our money was no longer in our piggy bank, but set aside for college. And while you are still in kindergarten, it is hard to imagine what college is, why it's important, or why you would need to save for it. Aside from the bank statements, the mail brought birthday and Christmas cards that sometimes contained a check or a five-dollar bill. So the arrival of mail became exciting because when an envelope was addressed to me, money was usually associated with it.

GRAPEFRUITS, GECKOS, AND GRASSHOPPERS FOR SALE

More than just a careful accountant, I was also a young entrepreneur. One enterprise involved an abundance of grapefruits. My uncle and his family lived on an old grapefruit orchard in Phoenix, Arizona. My family helped harvest the fruit, and my uncle encouraged Loren, my cousins, and me to sell them. We bagged them, set up a table, and posted a sign proclaiming "$5 a bag." My cousins and I sat at our little table, minding the grapefruits and waiting for the customers to start rolling in. We waited and waited and waited. No one stopped to buy our grapefruits. This is when I learned that old business saying, "location, location, location." In a neighborhood that used to be a grapefruit orchard, the people driving by were likely to have their own surplus of grapefruit.

The next day, we relocated from my uncle's house to ours, miles away from any orchards. We set up our table, posted the sign, arranged our bags of grapefruit, and waited to see what would happen. We sold every single bag that day for five dollars a bag.

Growing up, I sold lemonade, snow cones, pom-poms made

of yarn, and even geckos and grasshoppers that we caught. One of my more creative ideas was selling Tootsie Pops. We bought a bag of the lollipops and colored the bottoms of a few of the sticks red. I borrowed a bread basket from my mom, turned it over, and inserted the candy to hide the ends of the sticks. We sold the Tootsie Pops for fifty cents each and informed customers that if they picked one that was colored red on the end, they would get a second Tootsie Pop for free. My friends and I made a significant profit from all the neighborhood kids. Loren and his friends were especially receptive to these suckers.

When I grew older, I started babysitting, as a lot of other teenagers did. "Finally, I can make some serious money," I thought. At the time, I lived on a Navy base in Okinawa, Japan, in a neighborhood with a lot of younger children. My standard rate was a dollar per hour for each kid. From a couple with two kids, I could earn ten dollars a night. Soon, I began babysitting on a regular basis for several families in the neighborhood. My bank account and my wallet started to grow, and so did my spending power.

While living in Japan, we had a few different options for shopping. We could shop on the base at the Navy Exchange, or we could shop off-base, outside the gates. The exchange offered familiar items and brands, which was a nice convenience. But for an inquisitive teenager like me, shopping off-base was a lot more fun. It involved new and different products, and my dollar stretched a lot further. At the time, the exchange rate was around 250 yen to the US dollar. That meant I could buy twenty-five boxes of gum or candy, at ten yen each, with just one dollar. As a teenager, I was allowed to venture with my friends to malls outside the base. I had the money to make my own purchases, including earrings, bracelets, shoes, and cassette tapes. I enjoyed the independence of shopping on my own with money I had earned. I was accountable only to my notebook where I kept track of my income and outgo.

A MATCHING SAVINGS PLAN

My parents observed my increasing wealth and generously set up an incentive savings plan for me. For every dollar I deposited, they promised to add an additional fifty cents. You might be familiar with this concept. Many employers offer to match employee contributions to a company retirement plan. My parents may not have been prepared for me to make deposits of $50 at a time, bringing my total deposit to $75. Eventually, I accumulated $500, a small fortune for a thirteen-year-old.

My ability to save money came in handy when I later started driving. For my first few months as a driver, I had to ask my parents' permission to drive one of their cars, either a small, red hatchback or a big, blue minivan. I preferred driving the hatchback, but as every kid just starting to drive will tell you, having wheels beats walking any day of the week.

After driving for a year or so, I wanted to buy a car of my own. My dad found a silver hatchback similar to the one we already had, though just a few years older. In the end, my parents bought the silver hatchback and drove it. They sold me their red one because my dad wanted me to drive something more reliable than the slightly older model.

During this time, I was working evenings and weekends at a local fast-food restaurant, so I had some cash to put toward purchasing my car. My parents and I worked out a payment plan of $50 weekly installments until I had paid them $1,000. My brother Loren started driving while I was still making my payments. My parents thought it fair to have me share the red car with Loren until he bought his own car. Every other week, he got to drive the red car, and I was stuck using the minivan when my parents didn't need it.

The red car had a ten-gallon gas tank, and at the time gas was usually around a dollar a gallon. Ten bucks easily filled that tank. But often when we switched cars, very little gas remained in the tank. More than once, my brother tried to push the hatchback to the limit, running out of fuel blocks away from the gas station. As a result, my dad created a rule that on Sunday, when we switched cars, the hatchback needed to have at least a quarter tank of gas.

After I finished making payments on that car, I still had to share it with my brother. This was frustrating, but I supposed that I had to follow my parents' rules. Not long afterward, Loren finally bought his own car.

Owning a car, even a shared car, involved additional expenses that I had to determine. These included the weekly expense of gas and also maintenance costs like oil changes and replacement windshield-wiper blades. Still, hanging out with friends, going out for food, and seeing movies were important to me, and these activities cost money. I was earning more than I had been when I was just babysitting, but my expenses were higher now too. I had to learn to balance several priorities: having money in my pocket, adding to my savings account, and spending on food, clothes, and entertainment.

My schooling offered very little information to help me with this challenge. Many people feel that they don't know anything about money because they weren't taught in school or by their parents. In elementary school, you may have learned to identify the different kinds of coins and bills and the Founding Father on each. In high school home economics classes, you may have learned to balance a checkbook. In one of my high school history classes, my peers and I completed sample tax returns because the teacher believed that everyone should know how to do their own taxes. However, most of us learn the hard way how to handle our finances: We learn by seeing what works well for us and from mistakes we make. We can also learn by reading books and articles or talking to people we trust as money managers. Or we learn by watching our parents.

FAMILY VALUES

People often ask me how I got started in the financial industry. When I was younger, my father was the biggest influence on my understanding of and curiosity about money. He didn't grow up rich. Actually, he is one of eight siblings. His family lived in a modest home in a Phoenix, Arizona, suburb. My grandfather was in the printing business, and my grandmother often helped at the print shop.

Looking back, I feel fortunate that my father shared with me his stories and strategies for how he dealt with money. He also helped my mom's friends with their tax returns. A subscriber to *Money* magazine, he read it from cover to cover. He was the founder of his family's investment club and the treasurer for several years until it disbanded. At the library, he carefully researched companies for the club to invest in, such as Microsoft and Nordstrom, and sometimes I tagged along.

When my father was studying for his degree in business, he shared with me what he was learning. This included the idea that some companies, like Toyota, have a business model that you can follow for efficiency and success. I enjoyed our conversations tremendously and suspected that most of my friends didn't have these talks with their fathers.

Being in the Navy for twenty-three years didn't stop my dad from trying to find his pot of gold at the end of the rainbow. He and his two brothers started a company to make novelty coupon books. He crafted wooden games with pegs to sell to doctors' and dentists' offices. He believed that these games would save the offices money by reducing the number of magazine subscriptions they had to maintain. He mailed letters all over the area to introduce his products. He found a market for them, but not enough to quit his day job. Even though he was a career serviceman in the US Navy, he had the heart of an entrepreneur.

My mother taught me very different lessons about money. For her, it revolved around generosity and the abundance of food. If you ever walk into the home of a Filipino, more times than not the first question your host will ask you is, "Are you hungry?" Your answer had better be yes, or this person will keep asking or take your response as an insult. For my whole life, my mom has been feeding me. She is a fantastic cook famous for many of her dishes, Filipino and American. I recently met my youngest brother's former math teacher. She asked about my brother, and then about my mom. Ten years after my

As soon as I learned how to divide, my dad taught me the Rule of Seventy-Two. Albert Einstein is credited with popularizing this nugget of brilliance. You can use the Rule of Seventy-Two to judge an investment's potential. Divide the projected rate of return into seventy-two. The answer is the number of years required for the investment to double in value.

According to this rule, an investment that earns 8 percent annually will double in nine years (seventy-two divided by eight). So, if you invest $10,000 and you earn a hypothetical 8 percent on that investment, the Rule of Seventy-Two tells you that your investment could grow to $20,000 in nine years.

brother had left her classroom, she still remembered the *lumpia*, or Filipino egg rolls, that my mom brought to school on special occasions.

My mom is naturally generous. If I compliment her on a piece of jewelry she is wearing, she asks if I want it. Or it shows up as my birthday present. Like my dad, she comes from a big family—she has six siblings. When I was growing up, she would regularly send money orders back home to the Philippines to rebuild a roof after a typhoon or help pay for a relative's education. Sometimes the money was for my uncle who was working toward a degree in dentistry. Or it went to an aunt attending college to be a dietician. Even a cousin who was in school to be a merchant marine received funds from my mom. Whatever the need was, she found a way to help. She still sends money when her family needs it.

My mom didn't work outside the home much. For a few years while we lived in Arizona, she babysat some neighborhood kids. When we first moved to Washington State, she found a job at an electronic assembly plant that had a good dental plan, which would help cover the cost of the braces that Loren and I needed.

She found small ways to save money or stretch it. She made clothes for us. We clipped coupons and shopped for bargains. We always planted a vegetable garden in the backyard. There we grew a lot of the staples you find in American gardens and a few exotic vegetables or fruits my mom loved from her birthplace. She encouraged us to try new foods. We always had plenty to eat, and nobody was ever hungry.

Once, a young man selling Rainbow vacuum cleaners stopped at my parents' house. Something about him reminded my mom of Loren. She thought the salesman looked hungry and promptly fed him dinner. Another time, a friend of mine ended up on the same flight to Arizona as my parents and young nephew. She observed my mom pulling one snack after another out of her purse. She said my mom reminded her of Mary Poppins and her bag of goodies. Today, I make sure to pack extra snacks for a trip, and I cook more food than is necessary for every get-together. Just like my mom, I encourage my husband to try new foods. I strive to have her generous nature and look for ways to make little occasions more special.

MAKING SENSE OF MONEY

Children develop very different perspectives on money as they learn where it comes from and how it can be spent or saved. The value of money extends beyond the dollars and cents that we add to or subtract from in a checkbook register or investment statement. Most children don't keep a notebook as I did. Until they earn, save, and spend money, it remains an abstract concept. They find coins on the ground and in between seat cushions, so they believe that money is something found and not earned. Having money may feel like a matter of luck rather than a reward for hard work. Pennies can look like gold and appear to hold more value than they are actually worth. When asking for a toy or a pair of brand-name shoes, kids may hear, "We can't afford that" or "It's too expensive." Some don't ask because they know, or think they know, that their parents can't afford an item. Many kids spend their birthday money on inexpensive toys, while others save for a larger purchase. When children sell candy and other items to earn their own money, they may have to learn the hard way that their merchandise shouldn't cost them more than its selling price. Consider your own childhood money memories. Have you discussed them with your partner and examined how they might apply to your life now? We each learn about money through a combination of formal and informal education, lessons from our parents, and experiences. For many of us, this learning process includes the lesson that money is a taboo subject. But you and your partner must be able to speak openly about it.

As you two figure out how you will deal with your finances, discussing how you learned about money is helpful. Share interesting and funny stories from your past that describe situations that had an impact on you and helped shape your money personality.

Sunday brunch

....

Discover what part money has played in your partner's life. Share with your partner about your history with money:

- How did you obtain or earn money when you were younger?

- Once you earned it, how did you spend it?

- What are some of your childhood memories involving money?

- What do you remember hearing about money as a child?

- How does your experience compare with the way your parents, siblings, or friends deal with money?

LUMPIA SHANGHAI
From the kitchen of Amy Digges

For the lumpia

3 carrots

3 celery stalks

1 medium onion

1 eight-ounce can water chestnuts, drained

1 bunch green onions

4 large garlic cloves

2 pounds ground pork

A dash of salt and pepper

3 tablespoons soy sauce

Lumpia wrappers (can be purchased from an Asian grocery)

Vegetable oil

For finishing the dish

Sweet-and-sour sauce

A mixture of white vinegar, garlic, and salt

Chop the vegetables, including the garlic and onions, to a coarseness about the size of half a grain of rice. For the celery, chop them separately from the other vegetables and squeeze them to drain the liquid to prevent a loose mixture. Mix the vegetables with the meat, soy sauce, and salt and pepper in a large bowl. To separate the lumpia wrappers from each other, carefully peel them apart from each other. Enclose them in a dish towel to maintain their moisture. Work with one wrapper at a time, placing a pencil-width line of the meat-and-vegetable mixture across one side. Roll the lumpia tightly. Tuck in the ends, or leave them open. Repeat until you have wrapped all the meat mixture.

In a deep pan or fryer, heat one-half to three-quarters inch vegetable oil. The oil level should be just high enough to cover the lumpia. Place four to five lumpia at a time into the hot oil and cook until golden, turning the lumpia once. Cut the crispy lumpia in half or into quarters and serve with sweet-and-sour sauce or a mixture of white vinegar, garlic, and salt. Lumpia freeze well and can be cooked right from the freezer, without thawing.

3

....

A ROOM OF MY OWN

....

My first apartment was a fantastic little studio just north of Seattle. I moved an hour and a half from where all my family and friends lived to get out of that small town and to be nearer to the city. The apartment was new construction, complete with brand-new appliances. Its 550 square feet included space for a couch and a kitchen table, and a bedroom area large enough to house my childhood twin bed. Outside, I could grow flowers and strawberries on my little private deck. This studio was a wonderful place to call home and start my independence. My rent was $525 a month, just within my means.

I found a job in the home-electronics department of a large retailer and made just enough money most months to stay on top of my expenses. My parents gave me gifts of kitchen utensils, pans, dishes, and a microwave oven. What I didn't have—a TV, a vacuum cleaner, a new couch—didn't seem very important on this first venture into the world.

I enjoyed cleaning my home and keeping it tidy. After a while, I really missed having a vacuum cleaner. I regularly swept my carpet to round up crumbs and dirt. This seemed adequate for keeping my apartment clean, but I began to wonder what lurked under the surface of my swept carpet. I saved money and scoured the weekly ads for deals on vacuum cleaners. I finally found an entry-level Hoover on sale for sixty dollars. When I brought it home, I ran that vacuum over my carpet about a half-dozen times. I kept listening to the sounds of debris going into the bag. Who would have guessed that a one-month-old carpet used by just one person could hide so much dirt? Those were the days when I was absolutely content to spend my time off cleaning my little space completely, scrubbing and dusting from top to bottom and finishing with a run of the vacuum.

During my months without a TV, I didn't miss it. By not watching television, I had time to read or go out and get to know my new city. But then I was struck with baseball fever. That year, 1995, the Seattle Mariners won their first division championship and defeated the New York Yankees in the American League Division Series. I wasn't a diehard baseball fan, but Mariner fever had taken over the entire area. I started listening to baseball games on the radio, something I had never before done willingly.

In the home-electronics department where I worked, the other staffers and I would tune each television to the game. This not only drew in customers to watch Ken Griffey Jr. hit a home run or Randy Johnson throw strikes, it made it easy for me to catch up on the score. Finally, a nineteen-inch TV went on sale for $169, within reach of my meager savings. I brought it home and moved furniture around so it could sit on my dresser, across from the couch. I set up the antenna so I would be ready to watch the next Mariners game. Sitting at home alone celebrating the team's win was also a personal victory for me.

THE BUDGET CRUNCH

Working in retail, I discovered that my allotted work hours varied greatly from week to week. This put a lot of strain on my budget. I would lie awake at night mentally listing the bills I needed to pay. Numbers continually floated through my mind. Payments for my rent, phone service, student loans, and utilities left scant money for food, gas, and entertainment. I learned that if I couldn't fall sleep after a little while, it helped to get up and write out the list of expenses running through my head. Then, no longer afraid that I would forget to pay a bill or account for an unexpected expense, I could sleep. In the morning I could tackle the issues with a clear head.

When money got too tight, I started using credit cards to buy groceries and gas. I made payments to the electric company with my credit card because I didn't have enough in my checking account. This was my first lesson in how easy it is to buy with credit and how difficult it can be to pay off credit card debt. I remember when my store credit card reached almost a thousand dollars, and I realized that I couldn't keep managing my finances that way.

I took a second job to help fill the gap between my expenses and my income. I chose a position where I could stock shelves early in the morning for another retailer. This worked well for a few weeks until the Christmas season started. A problem arose when store hours were extended at my first job, lengthening my closing shift there. I would get home at around midnight or one o'clock in the morning and then have to get up at four thirty in the morning to go to my second job. I started sleeping through my alarm clock. When I woke up, my feet still felt tired. I realized that this wasn't working.

I called my parents to discuss what I should do next. I had

been trying to manage too much on my own. Approaching them was hard. Being able to support myself and take care of my own issues was important to me. But I was running out of ideas. The solution was a loan, which my dad co-signed, from our credit union. This loan was large enough to cover all three of my credit card balances and created a payment plan that I could manage. It took me two years to pay off that debt. The best part about this solution was that I was able to take care of my credit card problem without accepting any money from my parents.

While paying off my debt, I was promoted to the management-training program and quit my second job. My hard work earned me an assistant manager position in a great store. Things began to look up for me, and my finances became easier to manage. Even though I was making more money, I focused on living within my income.

I became very skilled at budgeting and saving small amounts on a regular basis for larger purchases. I deposited a small portion of every paycheck into a savings account at a credit union I didn't normally use. This was my emergency money. I purposely opened this account at a credit union where the nearest branch was far away. I had an ATM card to access that account when an emergency arose, but generally I tried to avoid dipping into those funds. To prepare for large purchases, I saved money in envelopes. This worked well for me because I could write what the money was for on the outside of each envelope. I could also record the date, the amount deposited, and the new balance and note any money that was taken out of the envelopes for other expenses.

A year later, to live closer to the city, I moved into a different apartment with two roommates. Having roommates made the urban lifestyle easier to afford. Their contributions to rent and utilities made my expenses much more manageable.

QUALITY CONTROL

When I was learning to handle my finances, I found it very helpful to write information down. I kept my bills and checkbook in one place. This freed me from obsessing over every detail and constantly wondering what I may have forgotten. When it was time to pay the bills, I knew what was due when and how that fit into my budget. Those experiences showed me that it's possible to make a budget work with less money; it just takes organization, creativity, and self-awareness.

Today many tools are available through software applications and websites. Finding the tool that works best for you can be hard. When I really need to buckle down and pay attention to the income and outgo, nothing works better than envelopes, a spreadsheet, or simply a pencil and paper.

Sunday brunch

- What financial successes have you experienced? What have they taught you?

- What tools or systems help you to be successful financially?

- Sometimes, we learn the most from our mistakes. What have you learned from yours?

4

"DAD, I HAVE A GREAT IDEA."

One day at work, the store director approached me personally to let me know that I was eligible for the company's 401(k) plan. Our conversation meant a great deal to me because she was someone I admired. She had worked for the company for a number of years and was preparing to retire earlier than she had originally planned. She said that I should contribute as much as I could toward the plan to receive the company's matching funds, virtually free money. She also told me that since I was young, I could be aggressive with my investments. If there was a downturn in the stock markets, I would have time to recover before I needed those funds for retirement, she explained.

I signed up for the 401(k) plan soon after talking to her and contributed as much as I could. I enjoyed reading the account statements and watching my investments grow. This process also started me thinking of retirement, the reason I was saving. During a phone call with my dad, I told him that I wanted to retire at age forty-five. This may have been naïve on my part because my father was about that age, had retired from the Navy, and was well into his second career. After putting two kids through college, and another one still to go, he was nowhere near able to retire. I am sure that he suppressed laughter. Outwardly, he only instructed me to save as much as I could.

In my early twenties, forty-five seemed a long way off. To me, retiring at forty-five didn't necessarily mean that I would quit working, but that I would have the financial freedom to do what I wished. So, I contributed as much as I could toward that goal. At times I ate ramen noodles so I could keep up my savings and 401(k) contributions. I was sure that if I kept advancing with the company and continued to save money, I could pull off my dream of early retirement.

In addition to saving money in my company retirement plan, I increased my contributions to my savings accounts. One benefit of living with roommates was that my expenses were lower for a time. I was also climbing the management ladder and bringing home a bigger paycheck. These changes allowed me to save even more.

During this time, I was expecting to transfer to a store in a small town closer to my parents' house. I believed that being a manager at that store would help me increase my retirement and savings contributions. I didn't necessarily want to live in that small town and hoped that I wouldn't have to for very long. But my lease for my apartment was expiring, and my roommates were going their separate ways. I talked with my parents, and when my lease ended, I moved into their house. In an unexpected turn of events, I ended up taking a management position in Seattle, and so made the long commute from my parents' home.

My move home was timely. My family and I seemed to need each other just a little bit more at that time. I had just broken off a poorly thought-out engagement. My baby brother was in middle school, and my mom and dad seemed to appreciate my needing them again. The unfortunate side effect was that I gained ten pounds enjoying my mother's cooking.

One morning during a particularly long commute to work, I called my dad and shared an epiphany with him: I wanted to buy my own house. I thought that I had figured it all out during the first half of my commute. He was supportive over the phone, but noticeably not as excited as I was. I recounted why I wanted to buy a house, how I was almost ready, and what I would do to get ready. I predicted that I could be ready to start shopping for a house in three years. That seemed like a fair amount of time to gather a down payment.

Though I paid my parents some rent to cover their extra costs of having me at home, I was able to save even more of my income toward my goal of owning a home. With every paycheck, I contributed to my 401(k), bought my employer's stock, and put money into my savings account. The only debt I had was my car payment.

After a year or so, I was motivated to move out of my parents' house again. Staying with them had been cathartic at first, and I was very grateful that they were there for me during a difficult time. Still, I was ready to go back out on my own—and shorten my commute—and I felt that I had enough money set aside to at least start looking for a new home to buy in Seattle. I worked with a real estate agent who showed me around and helped me decide if a house or a condo fit my needs better. The houses I saw were small and much farther away from Seattle than the condos were. I certainly liked the charm of a smaller house. Though I looked forward to using my own tools for little home-improvement jobs, I wasn't confident enough to tackle any major projects. A condo was a better decision for me because it required less maintenance and fewer upgrades. Buying a condo included the expense of homeowner's dues to take care of the landscaping and other outside maintenance. If I had purchased a house, that expense would probably have gone into maintenance of the house and yard. This seemed like a good trade-off.

Buying a home was a big decision for me. I had grown up in a military family that moved every few years. I had enjoyed moving often. When we stayed in one place a little longer than usual, I became restless. The itch to move would build until we finally did and settled into a new neighborhood. Naturally, when I was considering buying a home, the big question for me was, am I really ready for a thirty-year mortgage?

At the time, the 1990s, the Seattle housing market was growing strong, but wasn't as overheated as it became in the 2000s. I purchased an 1,100-square-foot condo with two bedrooms and one-and-a-half baths for $83,000. By comparison, one of my uncles had for the same price just purchased a house with three bedrooms, an office, and a pool in a Phoenix, Arizona, suburb. Still, I was happy with my new acquisition.

My family rallied around me to help update my new home. We replaced the original thirty-year-old shag carpet. We removed the tired molding. We scrubbed and peeled away the dated wallpaper borders that depicted kittens and flowers. We laid new vinyl flooring in the kitchen and bathrooms. My vision was a cozy interior that evoked the look and comfort of a warm cup of cocoa. I purchased a comfortable couch, love seat, and chair in a dark chocolate brown. I chose a creamy carpet with a hint of pink that reminded me of the foam atop hot cocoa, and a soothing milky color for the walls.

HOME-BUYING HANGOVER

The aftereffect of my new, cozy home was that I went into debt again. I had used a portion of my 401(k), all my stock, and part of my savings for the down payment. I had reserved some savings for a rainy day, but not enough that I felt comfortable using that money to furnish my home. Over time, my credit card debt had climbed to a daunting $7,000. Making home improvements, buying furniture that fit my new home, and purchasing a new computer had added quickly to my debt. I had been prepared for the cost of the new carpet, but the price of some of the other improvements had surprised me. I'd seriously underestimated the cost of moving and setting up my condo. Fortunately, my income was also higher than it had been in the past, so I could more easily repair the problem. This debt situation felt very different from when I moved into my first apartment and my expenses got away from me. I wasn't scraping by now. I could shift my priorities and where my income went. I felt that I could tackle this debt if I put a strategy in place.

My previous experience with debt had taught me many lessons: Debt has an uncanny ability to creep up and surprise you if you are not paying attention. It can feel like a weight that you carry around and can be difficult to shed. Debt drags down your net worth and sucks away your cash flow. Income that goes toward debt is money siphoned to past purchases. Especially if you are using credit cards to finance vacations, entertainment, or restaurant meals, what you enjoyed is in the past, and the future entails working to pay it off. To decrease your debt and shed the weight of it, you must divert more of your cash flow from saving for future goals. Some people can manage credit cards to maximize rewards like cash back and airline miles, but paying off the balance each month to prevent it from growing takes a great deal of discipline.

I was determined to apply these lessons. Recently, I had read an article about putting your credit cards on ice to remove the temptation to use them. In the case of an emergency or a golden opportunity, you must defrost them. The time this takes provides you a moment to consider

Don't worry, the ice doesn't usually damage the cards, and if it does, salesclerks can always key in your credit card number.

how urgent the emergency or how valuable the special offer is. And so I placed all my credit cards in a one-gallon plastic bag, filled it with water, sealed it, and stuck it in the freezer.

A couple of times after I had defrosted my cards, I was able to refreeze them without using them. After waiting for the ice to thaw, I had found that the urgency around those purchases evaporated. I stopped feeling compelled to rush out with my credit card and buy something impulsively. I explained this to a friend, and she said that she had used a similar method, except that she'd put the cards in a metal container, filled it with water, and then frozen it. That way, she couldn't use the microwave for a quick thaw.

As another part of my strategy to pay off my debt, I found a roommate. This was someone I had hired as an employee in the past and we remained friends. Because of our shared experiences, paying rent on time and keeping house was easy for us. Taking on a roommate helped reduce my expenses significantly so I could make larger payments on my credit card balance.

I also created a spreadsheet that listed the balance on each card, its interest rate, and the minimum payment. I calculated the total monthly amount that I could put toward the credit cards and prioritized them based on their balances and interest rates. I made minimum payments to some so I could pay off a few store credit cards with low balances, eliminating them from my list. Then, maintaining the same total monthly payment on my debt, I moved to the three remaining cards, which had larger balances. First, I targeted the card with the highest interest rate, paying as much as I could while making minimum payments on the other two cards. Once I paid it off, I shifted to the card that was the next highest priority. This process worked well for me, and I was able to get rid of all my debt fairly quickly.

While I was paying off this debt, I kept up my contributions to my 401(k) and savings account. I knew that if I delayed putting money into my 401(k), achieving my dream of early retirement would take longer and require more money later. I even returned to using envelopes to save for purchases for my home. I wanted to avoid using credit cards if possible. Having funds set aside from my paycheck, either in an account or in my envelopes, kept me on track with my savings goals and helped prevent me from accumulating credit card debt again.

CREDIT CARD PAYOFF STRATEGY

Current Debt	Personal Loan 1	Personal loan 2	Credit card 1	Credit card 2	Credit card 3	Credit card 4	Other loan	Other loan
Lender								
Balance								
Available credit								
Interest rate								
Minimum payment								
Current payment								

Payoff Strategy	Personal Loan 1	Personal loan 2	Credit card 1	Credit card 2	Credit card 3	Credit card 4	Other loan	Other loan
Lender								
Balance								
Minimum payment								
Current payment								
New payment								
Approxi- mate Pay off date								

Visit www.whenarealistmarriesanidealist.com for this and other resources.

THE REALITY CHECK

In hindsight, I can see how naive I was when buying the condo. But when I was working toward that goal, I felt unstoppable. Buying a home at such a young age taught me that if I focused my energies on an objective, I would inevitably achieve it and earlier than I expected. That is a powerful lesson for a twenty-four-year-old. The feeling of achievement and independence was intoxicating. In truth, I had enough savings for a down payment to buy the condo, but not enough to make it a home. I failed to consider the extra expenses. In the future, I would account for the funds needed to create the end result I sought and prepare for possible emergencies.

When I bought this home, I had hoped that my job would be

exciting and dynamic enough to pacify my wandering nature. That summer brought a great new opportunity for me. My employer chose me to be on the management team of its flagship store. Dreamer that I am, I saw only the benefits of this experience. But taking the position meant that I never spent much time in my incredible, beloved condo. My new job demanded more of my time than I wanted to share. For the most part, the only hours in which I occupied my condo were spent sleeping. I started taking days off just to sleep and do little tasks around my house. Had I known that I would end up working sixty-plus hours a week, that the knots in my neck would not disappear for years, and that the hiring environment would make it difficult for me to find good staff so I could have a life outside of work, I might not have taken that position. But then I would not have had the chance to meet the love of my life.

Sunday brunch

Buying your first home is a big milestone. Unexpected situations inevitably arise, and being prepared for them will help you feel more comfortable with your new investment. Consider and discuss the following questions with your partner before you buy:

- What resources do you have available already?

- What resources do you still need to gather?

- Who can you turn to for expertise and support?

- What can you afford (not what the bank will loan you)?

- What needs to be repaired or upgraded to make your new house a home?

- Are you prepared for the maintenance costs of your home?

- Plumbing fails. What will you do if yours requires unexpected repairs?

- Furnaces stop working, and clothes dryers quit drying. Do you know how much it will cost to replace each appliance, and do you have savings set aside for that eventuality?

5

....

YOU *CAN* TEACH AN OLD
GOAT NEW TRICKS

....

s I wrote this chapter, I found many occasions to fall in love with Rick all over again. He is a kind man and aims to please, though he finds it challenging to express his feelings. Naturally, I think he is wonderful. But even with our strong bond, arriving on the same page about money wasn't easy.

Growing up, Rick didn't think about money to a large extent until he started earning it. Finances were a sticky subject for his parents. His dad worked in the military while his mom stayed at home and took care of the kids and the house. Rick is still amazed that his parents provided for three children using what his dad earned from the Navy.

At age fifteen, Rick began working for his friend's dad in a cabinet shop. That was where Rick got his start in the carpentry trade. The shop manufactured and installed cabinets, store fixtures, and millwork for commercial and government buildings. Rick was paid two dollars an hour to work on Saturdays and weekdays during the summer. Sometimes he worked more when he needed to do installations at locations out of town. The job was a natural fit for Rick, who had spent many of his childhood years building tree houses with his buddy.

The first major purchase that Rick made with his new income was a stereo. For a while, he'd had his eye on a receiver and speaker set and looked forward to the days when he could play Led Zeppelin and Linda Ronstadt albums in the privacy of his basement bedroom. His junior year of high school, on the night before Halloween, he finally had enough money and the opportunity to make the purchase. Every penny he had at the time went toward the $714 price tag of that stereo. By December, he'd saved enough to buy the turntable to go with his new stereo. Buying this stereo was a milestone for Rick. Memories involving money—spending, saving, or losing it—would help shape his money personality, just as such memories do for others.

BEYOND TONKA TRUCKS

Rick often structures his personal story of money around cars he has owned. Sometimes he was impractical with money, and sometimes he managed it more sensibly. The way he spent money and how he decided on and rationalized the choice of a particular vehicle were signs of his financial situation and security at different points in his life. His options and financing and where he found each car were also telling.

A few years ago, Rick and I were watching a TV show in which a grown son visited his dad. In one scene, both men talked about a baseball game, its related statistics, and great past plays. In subtitles, this dialogue—seemingly about sports—was translated very differently: The son apologized for not appreciating his dad more.

The dad said how proud he was of his son. The men exchanged an "I love you." Rick and his son, Matt, have similarly layered conversations about cars. They seem to bond over exchanges about types of cars, how they handle, and their capabilities. Sometimes this language of cars has spilled into my relationship with Rick. I know an amazing number of trivial facts about cars. This has resulted from years of watching or listening to car shows and hearing Rick and Matt talk about different makes and models. So I am not surprised that for Rick, cars can represent certain times of his life and certain money situations.

Starting when he was a little boy playing with his Tonka trucks, he was particular with his means of transportation. When Rick was in high school, his dad gave him his old truck. It was a 1964 Ford F-250 Camper Special. It already had its share of scratches and dents, so Rick didn't worry a lot about keeping it nice. He could take it for a drive in the woods and squirrel around. The truck needed work, so Rick brought it to a shop to rebuild the engine. He tended to the suspension himself. Through this experience, he learned about the cost of maintaining a vehicle and the benefits of doing some of the work himself. The F-250 was a great truck throughout Rick's high school days.

A couple of years later, the shop that employed Rick moved forty miles north of where he lived. Rick thought it would be a good idea to find a car with better fuel economy than his old truck. His girlfriend's mom owned a Honda Civic, and he liked that it was small and nimble. He talked to the people at the Honda dealership and added his name to the waiting list. This was during the second oil crisis, in the late seventies, so there were waiting lists to buy many economy cars. He sold the truck for $1,500. Three months later, it was his turn to buy a Civic for $4,900. He had planned on using all his savings as a down payment. Instead, his dad and the loan officer at the credit union persuaded him to keep his savings for other emergencies and finance the whole cost of the car.

While Rick was in college, his girlfriend's brother, Erik, bought a 1967 Pontiac GTO. The muscle-car era had been a part of Rick's childhood. During high school, his favorite car had been a 1969 Ford Mustang Mach 1. Working on cars and rebuilding engines was fun for him. After he saw Erik's GTO and started helping him tune it up, he found that he wanted one too.

He came across an advertisement for a 1968 Pontiac GTO listed as a "mechanic's special" for $750. It had a manual transmission, which is desirable to gearheads like Rick. It didn't have air conditioning or many electrical options. The "old goat," as GTOs are often called, didn't run, but it was a two-door, red model with a black vinyl top. Rick paid cash and had it towed to his girlfriend's house. He didn't tell his parents about it until he had the car running a few months later.

Rick and Erik spent hours working on their two cars. They would swap out engines in the carport. They painted and tuned. Looking back, Rick says this may not have been the wisest way to spend his money. But considering the hours of enjoyment that car has brought him throughout twenty-five years of ownership, I would call it a good investment.

Rick's girlfriend ended up driving that car for a few years. Her own vehicle was a bare-bones 1970 Ford Maverick with a three-speed manual transmission that was hard to drive. It was the cheapest car that Ford made then. Rick rationalized the purchase of the GTO with the argument that his girlfriend wouldn't have to drive the Maverick. Even for him, spending or saving money is often an emotional decision, not a logical one. As many people do, he framed the purchase so it made sense and fit his understanding of his own money personality.

THE CHECKLIST

Rick believed that there were certain life objectives he should achieve, and in a specific order. He did everything he could to follow that order. He didn't know what his profession would be, but he knew that when he grew up, he wanted to be a father. Before he could do that, he needed to finish college, get married, and buy a house. So that is what he did. He graduated from college in 1984. The summer after he earned his degree, he married his high school sweetheart. After a while, they bought a house together. A year later they had Matt. Rick had a checklist in his head, and he ticked the items off one by one.

He had worked for the same little cabinet shop until a year after he graduated from college, when he was laid off and needed to find work. He had his degree in business, so he applied for operations and management jobs in the area. After a few interviews, he realized that he wasn't in his element. To start making money again quickly, he found a job working for a cabinet manufacturer. This kind of work was right up his alley.

Rick's financial situation felt steady again, so he and his wife started saving for a house. To do so, they decided to cut frivolous spending. For Rick, this involved eating in, keeping hand-me-down furniture longer, and thinking twice about large purchases. While they were saving money, they looked around every now and then for a house. They were motivated to move out of their one-bedroom apartment. Sadly, the high interest rates at the time were discouraging. But the next year, interest rates lowered and by that time they had saved a few thousand dollars.

They found a new house in a neighborhood they liked with a builder offering incentives for people interested in becoming homeowners. They got a Federal Housing Administration (FHA) loan, which enabled them to put only 3 percent down. Still, the down payment and closing costs ate up all their savings. But the builder, who was trying to sell homes quickly, included all the appliances and window treatments. Additionally, that builder had an arrangement with the lender to lower the payments, making it easier for first-time home buyers to get into a home. The builder bought their rate down to 8 percent the first year and 9 percent the second year as an incentive to get them into their house.

Usually after buying a house, growing used to the new mortgage payment takes a little while. As time goes on, making the payment becomes easier. Later that year, Rick became comfortable enough to buy a compact pickup truck. Not long after, he and his wife felt secure enough to start their family. Matt was born during their second year in that house.

Having established some security, Rick began looking at other career options. A friend of his from the cabinet-manufacturing shop had joined the carpenters' union. Months later, Rick joined, too, and went from earning $12.00 an hour to $15.40 an hour. At first, leaving the shop was scary. Through the shop, he had a guaranteed forty hours of work a week. By joining the union, he lost that guarantee but gained the opportunity to earn more.

During the early days of his union membership, he was generally employed by a fixture and installation company based out of Portland, Oregon. Retail stores were the majority of its clients. As a result, that first year Rick didn't work much between Thanksgiving and New Year's Day. This presented financial challenges that took some getting used to.

A couple of years after they added Matt to their family, Rick and his wife began to look for a larger, more comfortable car. They bought a 1990 Ford Taurus, which they later traded in for a minivan after five rebuilt transmissions in just four years. The minivan, a 1995 Dodge Grand Caravan, was loaded with options, including fourteen cup holders. It was roomier than the Taurus and fuel-efficient. But in the mid-nineties, for Rick, fuel economy was not the primary consideration in choosing a vehicle. Comfort was. The van had more options than any car or truck Rick had ever owned, even though it was a middle-of-the-road model.

A few years later, Rick and his wife split up. They went to counseling for a while, but ultimately it didn't help them work out their differences. The split was mostly amicable, so an attorney who was also a friend drew up their divorce papers. Rick sold the minivan and helped his soon-to-be ex-wife buy a Subaru. He kept his little pickup truck and the GTO. He also kept the house. They obtained three appraisals to determine its value and used the middle value as a basis for dividing that asset. He refinanced the house to settle the difference with her. She set herself up in a new place. The divorce was finalized in 1999.

While Rick was married, cash flow wasn't an issue. His wife paid the bills and worked part time. He feels that their individual approaches to their finances were more similar than his and mine are. After the divorce, his cash flow was still manageable. He found that he wasn't spending much, so he could put whole paychecks into his savings account.

Around this time, Rick and I started dating. I sometimes joke that I was the beneficiary of his midlife crisis. He claims that he didn't have a crisis. Yet the year that we began dating, he bought dirt bikes for him and Matt. Then he bought a newer, bigger diesel pickup truck—but only because I encouraged him to, he says.

THE REALIST IN ACTION

In general, Rick likes the feeling he gets from accumulating and saving money. For this reason, he sometimes shows an aversion to spending it. He will even put off replacing a basic appliance that isn't working. A couple of years ago, the fifteen-year-old TV in our family room started to fail. We began shopping for a new one. He spent quite a bit of time researching different technologies, brands, and sizes but didn't actually buy a TV then. Instead, the week before Super Bowl Sunday, he took it to a shop for repairs. New televisions are usually on sale before the Super Bowl, but he wasn't willing to part with the money then. We spent $300 on repairs on that old TV. A year later, something in him switched, and he felt comfortable buying a new high-definition TV. The old television now lives in my home office.

Our garage is full of tools that Rick has purchased over the years, and if a tool doesn't last two decades, he is disappointed. He knows all the little specialty shops around town that can fix his saws and drills. The receiver that he bought in high school still works and provides me with music in my office. It, too, has seen the repair shop a few times, but Rick can't bear to part with it. It is a miracle that he relegated it to the office. But since our new TV, cable, and video players have greater sound capacity, he felt that they called for a new receiver. If the new TV hadn't been high definition, I am sure he would have never replaced his old receiver.

Rick likes to extract the maximum value from each purchase. With that in mind, he doesn't buy a new car every few years, although there have been a few instances when it made sense to sell a car that was more hassle than it was worth. The vehicles that he uses daily he keeps for an average of ten years. He prefers cars that don't have all the bells and whistles. He likes those that are simpler, with fewer complicated parts that will need repair in the future.

Over the years, Rick has become more comfortable spending

money on himself—for instance, by buying parts for his cars. After his son was born, he had less time and money to get his cherished '68 GTO running as he wanted. Now, when he earns money from side jobs, he sets it aside for that project. He calls this his mad money. Still, he doesn't always find it easy to spend the cash.

He used to joke that when Matt got his driver's license, it would be a good time to take the transmission out of the GTO and fix the car up. That way, if Matt were tempted to take it out for a spin without permission, he couldn't. For years, I have encouraged Rick to take that mad money and invest it into his car. We both enjoy weekend trips in it. This year, seven years after Matt got his license, Rick is finally taking my advice. The transmission has been rebuilt. He has removed the engine to repair a persistent oil leak and clean it up. He is replacing the headers. At the end of this project, he may even repaint the car.

Throughout our relationship, Rick's love of saving hasn't stopped him from surprising me every now and then. For my birthday a couple of years ago, I wanted to buy a new dress. I went shopping and found two that I liked equally. I tried them on several times at the store. I asked the clerks for their opinion, but I still couldn't decide. I bought them both so I could ask Rick what he thought and then return the other one. I tried on the dresses for him, and he liked them a lot. To my delight, he encouraged me to keep them both.

Sunday brunch

As we go through life, it often feels that we are supposed to achieve certain goals—for example, attending college, getting married, buying a home, having children, and then retiring at age sixty-five.

- Are you living your life the way you are supposed to or the way you want to?

- When have you taken a risk that paid off? When has your risk-taking been a foolish mistake?

- Things don't always turn out the way you had planned, but you adapt. What are examples of compromises you have made when events didn't go according to plan?

6

COHABITATION

Gradually, one dresser drawer at a time, Rick and I learned to be comfortable in each other's space. Once I started spending more and more time at his house, I would leave things behind to make my next visit easier. I started by leaving a toothbrush and a contact lens case. Still, I didn't want to intrude on his life or space too much. I purchased a very small alarm clock. I bought a box with a lid to enclose the alarm clock and the other miscellaneous items that tend to end up on the nightstand: glasses, jewelry, makeup, even my nightly read. For a time, my clothes dryer quit working, and I did my laundry at my parents' house. When I was at Rick's, I could shop the laundry basket in my trunk for items to wear the next day. I could have done laundry at Rick's, but I didn't want to impose before he was more committed to our relationship.

After we had the Money Talk and agreed to live together, the process of actually moving in took place trunk load by trunk load, until only the furniture remained. Rick felt secure about our decision because I kept a place of my own, my condo. We had decided to try renting it out instead of selling it. I guess he thought that if our relationship didn't last, I would have someplace to go.

My moving into Rick's house made sense because that was where we spent most of our time together. Most of all, this option would be less disruptive for his son, Matt. I don't recall that we ever even considered moving into my condo. I don't think Rick spent one night there. Now, I probably wouldn't recommend moving into someone else's space. We did it to keep Matt's home life stable. A temperamental teenage boy can handle only so much jostling.

THE LANDLORD'S LAMENT

At the same time that I moved in with Rick, I became a landlord. We tried to fix up the condo so that a renter couldn't do that much damage. Luckily for me, I was now living with a finish carpenter. We replaced the floor in the bathroom and the existing tub and shower surround. We used a lot of caulk to fill in the gaps. We double-checked all the appliances to make sure they were working properly and repainted and installed baseboards. We replaced the screen door that was falling apart. I investigated the right amount of insurance to cover the condo. I found a company that would do credit checks on potential tenants then listed my condo for rent.

Through the process of renting out the condo, we learned that Rick doesn't like being a landlord. I relied on him as my handyman, and he dislikes people who don't take care of things. He didn't necessarily expect tenants to fix items that broke, but he did expect a timely call so we could take care of problems. We received a call one day from my tenant saying the water heater was leaking. When we arrived to investigate, water had seeped into the carpet and padding all the way into the living room and throughout the dining room. The tray in which the water heater sat was cracked. Instead of collecting in the tray and swirling down the drain, the water had soaked into the floor. The tenant's daughter had just had a baby, so she had only recently gotten around to calling us, three days after she first noticed the water.

Several years later, when she moved out, we faced a similar situation. The upstairs bathroom floor had been damaged by water over time, and Rick had to replace it again. He complained about fixing things that should not have needed fixing. We painted and had the carpets cleaned in preparation for a new tenant. Unfortunately, at that time, it was much harder to find one. There were two other units in my complex for rent, and mine was the most expensive. Moreover, many would-be renters were buying homes instead.

Still, once we were living together, everything seemed a little easier. I was more comfortable settling into the couch to watch a movie knowing that I didn't have to drive home at the end. Matt could see that I wasn't going anywhere and that we would have more time to get used to each other. Cooking dinner was more enjoyable with others to share the meals and help clean up. Sharing the financial burden of housing, a cost that takes up a third to a half of many people's income, decreased both of our expenses. I was able to further build my savings in case of a lapse between tenants. But the largest benefit was affirming our compatibility and seeing how we worked through difficulties, how each of us could give and take in a loving and respectful way. Plus, figuring out what to wear the next day was a lot easier now that all my clothes were in one place.

Once, months before, I had worn a sweater over a tank top

while visiting Rick. I had planned ahead and brought my clothes to wear to work the next day. As I was dressing the following morning, I realized that I had not packed a bra. Later at work, I was walking from my department back to my office and took a shortcut through the freezer aisle. I felt a chill and wondered, "If someone noticed and said something, would that person be guilty of sexual harassment? And could I somehow be at fault too?" The company dress code specified which items of clothing were necessary, and a bra was one of them. Thankfully, now that Rick and I were living together, I didn't have to worry about those kinds of details anymore.

ROOM FOR IMPROVEMENT

Though we took our time reaching this step, Rick and I probably could've been more thoughtful about our move in together. We figured out the logistics of paying bills and creating a joint account for home expenses, but we failed to talk about some important issues before the move. I would have liked to ask him the following questions then: How will we decorate your house with our combined belongings? Do you have a budget for paint, drapes, and other little comforts that will cost money? Who will do which chores? How should we handle unexpected expenses associated with your home or the condo? And, especially, do we have to keep the gigantic, ugly, blue recliner that your friend left when he moved to Alaska? The idealist in me thought that love would take care of all the details.

When I moved into Rick's house, we did do a few little things to make it cozier. We replaced his broken-down couch in the family room with mine. We painted the master bedroom. Matt became the beneficiary of my television and VCR. Rick and I comingled our music and video collections and hung some of my artwork. I started planting flowers and vegetables in his yard. In my former apartments, I had often experimented with growing plants, especially those that are good to eat. The condo had a great deck and plenty of sunshine that made it perfect for growing stuff. While living there, I had planted strawberries, watered them, and left them to do their thing. I'd continued to water them when I could, but the strawberries struggled. When my mother and her green thumb came over, she offered tips and brought fertilizers. Still, my strawberries were marginal. I felt doomed to a life of store-bought berries. My mother's family consisted mostly of farmers, and I was sure that I had inherited some of those genes. So at the time I didn't understand why I couldn't grow big, juicy, luscious strawberries.

It turns out that plants require a little more than just soil and the occasional watering. My strawberry plants didn't grow because I was never around to tend to them. Weeds need pulling, runners need pinching, and plants need fertilizer. I learned this when I started gardening at Rick's house. After I moved in, I started planting good things to eat again. My need to get my hands dirty and to watch something grow must be instinctual. I planted a full pot of strawberries and filled another with fresh herbs. I scattered sunflower seeds and tomato starts along the south wall of the house. Amazingly, these plants grew.

It took me awhile to figure out what I had done differently with these plants. Then I realized that I was spending a lot more time at home to be with Rick. This also meant being around the plants I had always wanted to grow and then eat. Having a black thumb had never been my problem; I simply hadn't been present to take care of my plants.

In the house where we live now, I have two large raised beds, an herb garden, and a pea patch. My garden is beautiful, especially in the summer. It provides me with raspberries, strawberries, zucchini, beans, peas, herbs, and lots and lots of fat, juicy tomatoes.

WHO TAKES OUT THE TRASH?

Couples choose to move in together for many reasons. Sharing a living space may be convenient, make financial sense, or serve as a test of readiness for marriage, for example. Living together before marriage has become more socially acceptable than it was in the past, but that doesn't make it easier. Sometimes complications arise. Once you and your partner decide to share a home, other decisions follow: Will you move into one of your existing homes or find a new one? How will you manage your financial obligations? Some couples add up all their household expenses, divide that sum, and share the financial responsibility, for instance, by one partner writing checks to the other. Contributing a percentage to a joint account for household expenses also works. Other couples divide up responsibility for specific bills, one partner paying the rent and the other paying for the utilities and food. Some who move in with their partner before marriage consider making a relationship or cohabitation agreement, which is a formal agreement containing details of ownership.

Next comes the coordination and planning of the move. What do you do with extra couches, beds, and dining room tables? How will you decorate your new place to incorporate your individual styles? Will you each put your name on your CDs and books to clarify ownership in case your relationship sours? Cooking together, sharing a bathroom, and spending a lot more time together can present new challenges. Does each of you have a place to retreat to when you need to be alone?

The timing of next steps in a relationship varies a lot from one couple to another. Some move in together after just a few months; some wait a lot longer, as Rick and I did. My parents married after knowing each other for just two months. Moving in together requires a lot of love and respect from both partners. Aside from the financial implications, you both must resolve compatibility issues to make it all work. Most barriers between you and your partner will dissolve when you move in together. If you have ever shared a bathroom sink with someone else, you understand this. Men leave whiskers all over the sink and counter. Women usually take up a lot of real estate on a bathroom counter with bottles, gels, and potions to keep their hair and skin young and healthy. Finding room for hairdryers, curlers, and straightening irons can challenge the space available in many bathrooms. At the commode, men are infamous for their aim, or lack of it. Not knowing whose hair is clogging the drain or whose toenail clippings missed the wastebasket adds to the gross-out factor and tension in a shared bathroom.

Grocery shopping and cooking in the same kitchen can be challenging as well. Fortunately, Rick and I didn't have to fight over whether to buy Miracle Whip or mayonnaise. But other food items were divisive. His pantry was stocked with Rice-A-Roni and instant potatoes. Since I am half Asian, I prefer plain rice with just a little soy sauce. I used to make it in a little rice cooker that was a gift from my mom when I moved out. I had a hard time accepting rice mixed with pasta and other flavors in a box. But I thought that maybe this dish was a staple for Rick, a single dad.

When you first move in with your partner, cooking and cleaning can seem like a new romantic adventure. I showed Rick the deliciousness of homemade mashed potatoes, which really don't take that long to prepare. He made macaroni and cheese from scratch and baked it in a casserole dish. Previously, I had eaten only the kind that came in a blue box. After a while, the particulars of what your partner won't eat, or what he or she can't seem to stop eating (tacos for dinner again?), can start to get old, but you make allowances. When cleaning the house, you stake out the chores you prefer to do. I dust because I don't mind doing it, and Rick follows with the vacuum. We divide up the bathrooms, declutter each room, and a couple of hours later the house is shiny again.

Among shared spaces, closets can be a touchy topic for couples. Since I have known Rick, he has weeded out-of-date or worn-out clothes from his closet only once. He refused to get rid of a dozen sweaters that he received as gifts and never wore. He is still holding on to a pair of ugly shoes from the eighties. While I was moving in with him, I was motivated to help him make room in his closet. This closet was half the size of my former closet, and I had to share it with him. Our closet now holds three to five shirts that he wears regularly in the winter and three to five that he wears mostly in the summer. Even though he wears only those few shirts, our closet is jammed with clothes: tired, worn-out shirts that he hasn't eliminated and newer ones that he hasn't worked into regular rotation. I don't get worked up about this situation anymore because I have enough space for my clothes. Apparently, I can't help him donate a few shirts any more than I can help him let go of ugly, old shoes he hasn't worn in the past decade. His reason for holding on to things is that they may come back in style or that they are classic, which they aren't.

Other aspects of our living arrangement that Rick liked could have been different had we been married. He liked that he wasn't responsible for maintaining my car. When I washed it, he sometimes helped me reach the roof, but I did the rest. I took care of my own oil changes and other wear-and-tear items. He liked that we made small changes to improve the look and feel of his house.

Even couples who wait until marriage to live together must navigate similar situations. Figuring out whose furniture fits where, sharing spaces and responsibilities, and learning new habits are part of the romance and the challenge of occupying the same home as your partner.

GETTING ORGANIZED

....

Factors to consider before you move in together:

- The more you communicate about moving in before acting on your plans, the easier the whole process will be.

- Starting in a new place together is easier than one of you moving into the other's home. Is that an option you can consider?

- Identify the belongings that really matter to you. Keep the fabulous couch you scrimped and saved for, but let go of the beat-up coffee table you inherited from your brother.

- Coordinate what you will and won't keep. Create a plan to sell or donate duplicates or items that don't fit your shared home.

- Discuss what each of you requires to be comfortable in your shared space. Fresh paint, throw rugs, and accessories can be inexpensive ways to decorate so you can both enjoy it.

- Identify pet peeves, like clutter or a greasy stovetop, and address them. For example, I enjoy doing laundry, but I hate folding socks. I will tend to the laundry as long as Rick folds his socks.

- Keep your finances separate until you are married. Consider using a joint account to handle household expenses, like rent and utilities.

7

ADVENTURES IN
BUYING FURNITURE

As Rick and I adapted to sharing space, we also made the transition to sharing more of our time. I was still a manager in a large retail store. That meant that I worked odd and long hours. Some days the only quiet time that Rick and I enjoyed was right before going to sleep. I would start asking questions about his day or tell him about mine. Each time, he wanted only to sleep. We could have had these discussions over dinner, but even when I was home in time for the meal, we usually ate in front of the television. Hours in front of the TV didn't feel like quality reconnecting time after a day apart at work. Though I completely understood Rick's need for sleep—we both started our days early—I was missing a time when we could relate our daily happenings. I couldn't pinpoint a more appropriate hour to chat. Finally, I decided that the solution was not so much a matter of timing as it was a matter of furniture—particularly, a new dining room table.

For me, a new dining room table was the cure. We could lose weight and get healthier by being more intentional when eating dinner. Rick, Matt, and I could sit and talk about current events and happenings at school and be the picture of a blended family making it work. I could improve my relationship with Matt by dazzling him with my cooking skills and having this time to share. I truly thought that the table would be the solution to everything.

The existing dining table at that time belonged to Rick's ex-wife, who didn't have room for it in her home. So it sat in ours, though it was too big for the space. It left barely enough room for the chairs, let alone people to sit in them. This large, flat object ended up collecting projects, homework, and leftovers from the day. Of course we ate in front of the TV; the dining room table obviously was not the place to eat and converse.

We spent several weekends looking for just the right replacement. We debated whether Rick should make a table or whether we should buy one. Rick creates beautiful furniture when he has the time and motivation. In some cases, store-bought tables made of certain materials can be cheaper than a handcrafted one. But all the tables we saw at the store were too big, too small, or not nice enough. The longer we shopped, the more impatient I became. One Saturday, we walked into a store that was having a retirement sale. We'd never noticed this store before, though we often drove through the surrounding area. As soon as we entered, a beautiful cherry wood table for six caught our eyes. I tried to be nonchalant while we roamed the rest of the store. But I kept glancing at the table and then at Rick to see if he shared my interest. Finally, a salesman approached and asked us if we had any questions. Rick started asking about the cherry table! He seemed impressed with the quality of construction, and we both loved the color and depth of the wood.

This cherry table was almost perfect for our current house or a new one. We both love cherry. The table was a nice size. The only drawback was that it didn't have a leaf to expand it for larger gatherings. That feature hadn't been important to me when shopping for a cheap little table, but this was real furniture that we could keep in our house for a long time and use to serve Thanksgiving dinners. Early in our search, I had pictured a small, round table with leaves that we could push up against a wall when just the two of us were dining. I'd imagined that we wouldn't spend too much on such a table because we might not need it in the new house that we would purchase after we got married. (We were not engaged yet, but I was thinking ahead for both of us.)

Because the store was going out of business, there was a significant markdown on the table. We hadn't discussed a budget for this item or talked about what amount we would each contribute toward the purchase, but the cost was more than I had expected us to spend. I wondered, if we bought the table and Rick contributed more than I did, would I feel comfortable with the item? I was not certain that both of us were committed to sitting at the table for dinner. What would happen if we didn't buy this table? I asked myself. Would I keep trying to reach out to Rick while he was distracted and create more division in our relationship? Would this be the end of our relationship, the point at which we went our separate ways, or could we find another solution to this problem? Was I being too dramatic in my thinking because this table was so beautiful?

We walked out of the store to think about whether to make the purchase. This was my first lesson in how Rick buys furniture and makes decisions about large purchases. It was also the first time that I had ever shopped for furniture with a man other than my father. I know now that Rick needs to leave the store to think about a purchase. He takes time to internally process the information he has received. As a finish carpenter, he is especially selective when buying furniture. I have learned that he buys cheap items because of how he will use them or he buys something he can fix up. Alternatively, he buys very nice, heirloom-quality furniture. At the time, his house held a mix of these purchases: garage sale finds that he had refinished and heirloom pieces that he had purchased or inherited.

Standing outside the store, I didn't know these things about his decision-making process. I couldn't tell what he was thinking since he kept his feelings to himself. Because we had left the store without the table, I felt that the whole idea was lost. To Rick, this purchase represented hours that he had worked and saved. He needed to justify why we were buying this table instead of using the one that was already in our dining area. He was asking himself, if we bought this table, would he really want to sit for dinner and have a conversation? And if things didn't work out for us, would this piece of furniture be another relic of a relationship gone awry, like the current dining room table? Then there were the details of dovetailed joints, types of finishes, and where the table had been made. To be sure that it would fit in our space, he had measured it with the chairs tucked in and pulled out as if people were sitting in them. Rick kept these thoughts and measurements in his head until the pieces all clicked into place and he was ready to decide.

My decision-making process followed a different course then, as it does now. When I find a need for something, I generally picture a few different variations of that item with the features that I want. While shopping, when I see an item that matches the image, features, and budget I have in mind, I make my purchase. I have already made the decision long before I hand over the cash. To some, my decision may seem hasty. But by the time I make a purchase, I have already spent a significant amount of time thinking of the various options and preparing to spend the cash. For me, money represents the ability to enjoy things that I find important, like conversations over tasty dishes I have prepared with family and friends gathered around. Clearly, Rick and I have very different decision-making processes for spending. Neither way is right or wrong. Still, the result at that moment was that we did not go home with a new dining room table.

We drove home in silence that day. Instead, I would have liked for us to have a conversation like the following:

"I really liked that cherry table, but it is more than I thought we would spend. What do you think, Rick?"

"I'm glad that you brought up that it is more than you thought we would spend. How much did you think you would put toward the purchase?" he would ask.

I'd reply, "I was thinking that since it would be more of a small, casual table than a full-size dining room table, I would contribute as much as $300. I thought that would be more than enough for a simple table that would sit in a high-traffic area, like the maple one we saw at the first store. I didn't think we would both fall in love with such a nice dining room table."

"Yeah, I like the wood, the finish, and the craftsmanship of the cherry table. I know we were looking for an inexpensive table to fit into that space, but the cherry table caught my eye as soon as we walked into the store. The more I looked at it, the more I liked it. I see your point about the maple table from the first store, but I'm not as excited about buying a table with veneers. The cherry table costs more than I thought I would spend. But the store has already reduced the price significantly, and if you contribute, I would be willing to take care of the rest."

"Since the owners are closing the store and trying to sell everything, I wonder if they would be willing to negotiate the price. Maybe we can get the table for an even lower price if we take it with us and they don't have to deliver it."

"Yes, the table would be an even better value if they could do that. Are you sure you like the table, Stacy? Will you still like it as much if we don't split the cost fifty-fifty?" Rick would ask.

"I really like that table. It looks like the kind of piece we can build a room around. I love the warmth of the wood, and the size is perfect. For me, splitting the cost fifty-fifty is not important—picking the piece out together and creating family time are. If you are fine with covering a majority of the cost, I will give you the $300. Are you ready to go back to the store?"

"Yep. I'll turn around."

In reality, when we finally did speak about the decision, the conversation didn't go so smoothly. I had to ask a lot of questions to draw out where Rick was in his process. I deliberately waited for his responses to my questions. I had to quell any hysterical reactions that I may have been considering to allow for a reasonable, rational conversation. I sat at his ex-wife's table to confirm how uncomfortable it was. I tried to let go of my attachment to the cherry table since the result I wanted, quality family time, did not depend on which table we chose, so long as we had space to sit together. I asked Rick to consider his options out loud so I could hear what was happening in his head.

We discovered that he was comfortable contributing a majority of the money, and I was comfortable not doing so. I also realized that our relationship would not end if we didn't buy this table. He recognized that having time to discuss our days was really important to me, that I needed to understand what was going on in his life, and that I appreciated him showing curiosity about mine. We committed to eating as a family and investing in this table. Upon returning to the store, we found that the owners were indeed willing to negotiate the price if we took the table with us then. Rick's ex-wife made room for her table. I learned that Rick was much more open to conversation when food and music lubricated our discussion. He learned how much I enjoyed cooking and entertaining.

Over the years, we have successfully bought many pieces of furniture. Most of those decisions involved a process similar to this, but with more ease. That first experience taught us how we each approach decisions to buy. The main lesson is that we were able to make this decision together while keeping each of our preferences in mind. Rick has learned that sometimes he needs the extra push from me to make a decision, and I have learned a little patience.

And Thanksgiving, which has always been one of my favorite holidays, continues to be great, partly because of our cherry wood table. I've always loved planning the guest list, side dishes, and dessert, but the tricky part of hosting twenty or more people is seating them all. Rick and I like the feeling of having everyone at one table, so we have refined our seating arrangement to include the use of our cherry dining table and a well-built table made of scrap lumber, complete with leaves. Once we throw matching tablecloths over them and add place settings, candles, and flowers, they look beautiful. Then we can all sit down, say grace, and enjoy the bounty.

GETTING ORGANIZED

....

Try these tips for a successful large purchase:

• Understand the features and benefits that you are looking for in that particular item.

• Communicate why you want the item and what you hope to get from it.

• Talk about possible outcomes. For example, it may take time to find the right match, the item may be on backorder, or one of you may change your mind.

• Create a budget acceptable to both of you and become familiar with any return policies.

• Respect your different decision-making processes.

• When shopping, allow yourselves time away from the sales floor for a private discussion.

8

"yes, Yes, YES! (It's about time.)"

Rick proposed on May 3, 2002, at Cannon Beach, Oregon. We had driven there for a long weekend. That coastal town has been a special place for us ever since we spent our first weekend away there. During our visit in 2002, we took a leisurely drive farther down the coast to look at the farm Rick's grandparents used to own. We took our time driving back up the coast and stopped for a closer look at roadside curiosities. Then we headed to the restaurant at our hotel for a late dinner. As we sat down to dinner, I had a brief feeling that Rick might propose. But several months before this, I had resigned myself to the idea that he wasn't ready to marry yet. Therefore, my feeling about a possible proposal was fleeting. And in fact the proposal didn't happen during dinner—it happened later that night.

After an enjoyable meal, we went to our room to sip wine by the fireplace and look out over the beach toward the ocean. After some snuggling and kissing on the couch, Rick reached for something between the cushions. He pulled out a small jewelry box. I tried not to get overly excited. Sometimes a small jewelry box holds a necklace or earrings instead of a diamond ring. Prying the box from the couch had already put Rick on his knees. When he opened the box and I saw that solitaire diamond ring, he didn't even have a chance to ask me the question. I wrapped my arms around him and said, "Yes, yes, yes." Tears welled up in my eyes, and I leaned back to see his expression of nervous relief. He took the ring out of the box and gently slid it onto my finger.

I had been ready for this moment much sooner than he had been. Long before he finally made the leap, I had come to the decision that he was the one and only for me. For a time, I had even considered proposing to him, but that may not have accomplished the same goal. So I had prepared myself to wait until Rick was ready so I would know that we were both sure about taking this next step. My feelings while waiting for his proposal recall some lines from the movie *When Harry Met Sally*. Billy Crystal, as Harry, runs to Meg Ryan, as Sally, on New Year's Eve. He says to her, "When you realize that you want to spend the rest of your life with somebody, you want the rest of your life to start as soon as possible." I just wasn't able to get Rick to the same place where I was at the same time.

The year and a half I spent waiting for him to propose felt like a very long time. At one point, I almost gave up the expectation that he would ever propose. I know other women who have waited longer and some who tired of waiting, gave up, and ended a relationship. Now that Rick and I are married, it is easier for me to look back and appreciate why it took him so long to reach the same place where I was. Even then, I understood why he was holding back from taking that next step. Still, the wait was hard while we were in the middle of it because I was so caught up in my own feelings.

After Rick's two-year separation and divorce, he'd had difficulty believing that he'd found love again so quickly with me. For a while, he hadn't been sure if he was staying with me just to fill the void, if this was a rebound relationship, or if it was the real thing. He hadn't had a chance to date much, so that also gave rise to some doubt. A couple of times, I'd invited him to go out and date all the crazy women who are out there, but I'd quickly changed my mind. He was worried about the effect a second marriage could have on his son, Matt. Also, if our marriage didn't work out, divorce always has an impact financially. It would mean having to start over again.

Recently, I asked Rick what made him finally decide to propose. He told me that he knew because something inside clicked and he realized that I was the one person he wanted to be with the rest of his life. He had been aware that I was waiting and that this was the next step of our relationship.

Clearly, the decision to marry is one that each person has to reach in his or her own time. In my relationship with Rick, it made sense for me to wait for him to be ready. Yes, I was impatient, but I was in this for the long haul, so I demonstrated that by waiting for him to come to the decision on his own. It is a stereotype that men are afraid of commitment. Rick didn't fear commitment. He likes being married. He let me know that early in our relationship. He enjoys having someone there to share his life. Now we enjoy a level of comfort and security that I never knew before getting married.

WHEN TWO BECOME ONE

When I talk to unmarried couples who are living together and the subject of marriage comes up, some say that they believe everything will remain the same after they get married. This can lead them to put off the decision to marry. In my experience, everything changes once you are married. This change isn't just the result of the legal bonds that tie you together, though they do offer certain protections and security. The change is also the effect of standing together and pledging to God and all your friends and family that you have found the person who makes your life complete. Promising that you will do everything you can to make that person happy for the rest of his or her life and hearing your partner do the same has an overwhelming impact.

If you are living with your partner but are not married, you have to act differently to protect yourself in the event that your relationship doesn't last. It is important to keep yourself financially separate, such as with individual accounts. Some couples will open a joint checking account to pay for household bills, but the majority of your personal finances should remain under your own control.

A BUDGET-CONSCIOUS WEDDING

I felt a shift in my relationship with Rick immediately after his proposal. During the remainder of our weekend in Cannon Beach, I was on cloud nine. We held hands and kissed at every opportunity. All the difficulty, indecision, and doubt felt resolved. Ideas and plans for the wedding drifted into and out of my head. I knew that this proposal had changed everything; I just didn't know exactly how.

We agreed that we didn't want to go into debt for the wedding. The important thing for us was to have a day when all our friends and family could join us in this celebration. We wanted it to be more than a big party, though. We believed that people would remember this day because they were able to share in our love and because we were able to share in their well wishes. We resolved to keep it informal and fun. Then we started saving money and researching our options.

Like me, most brides have never planned an event like a wedding, and hope to never have to do so again. I felt incredible pressure to create a wonderful and magical day that was unique, personal, and memorable for the two of us and our guests. Fortunately, caterers and wedding venues host open houses where a bride and groom can check out their facilities and taste the fare they offer. Also, at wedding shows a couple can find virtually everything they need for their wedding. In fact, we found our venue, the minister, the photographer, and even my wedding dress at one wedding show where I dragged Rick and my parents. I bought books and questioned friends who had recently tied the knot. I spent hours on the Internet researching how to plan a wedding. I was afraid that the day would arrive and I would realize that I had completely forgotten an obvious detail. I made and remade lists and asked friends to help pull all the details together.

Getting started on the actual plans was hard. But once we selected the venue and my dress, everything else seemed to fall in line. We decided to get married at an old farmhouse that had been refurbished for just this sort of thing. My dress was last season's, but fit in with the casual setting of the farmhouse and the informal feel we wanted.

We decided to foot the bill for the wedding ourselves. Traditionally, the bride's parents pay for the reception, which can be a large part of the total cost of a wedding. Since my parents had one son in college and another ready to start college soon, it didn't feel right to ask them to pay for our reception. Besides, if my parents had paid, the guest list easily would have been twice as long or more. Rick and I both felt comfortable with this decision since we were independent and this was Rick's second marriage. Also, paying for the event allowed us more say in the wedding details. The idealist in me felt that with a little creativity we could pay for the whole event, and the realist in him saw this as the only logical option available to us. Even though I was the idealist in this scenario, I had a little bit of that pragmatic nature. And although Rick was the realist, he wasn't so unromantic that he wanted to get married at city hall. We felt that this easy decision was the right way to begin our lives as a married couple. We determined that if my parents or his mom wanted to contribute, they could, but the majority of the expense and decisions would be ours.

We have a lot of family living near our home and around the country. If you include all of my mom's friends whom I call "auntie" and "uncle," the list is even longer. Creating a guest list that would fit our venue and catering budget and include everyone was difficult. Our goal was to have no more than one hundred people attend the wedding and we sent out eighty-eight invitations to family, friends, and a few coworkers. We knew that some would come alone, some would come with a plus-one or their whole families, and some wouldn't be able to make it.

When we created our budget, we knew that catering and the venue would be a large part of our expenses. As we added the other necessary expenses, I insisted on spending more on the photography since that is what we would keep after our wedding day ended. To compensate for what we would spend on catering and the photographer, we enlisted the help of friends and family in keeping other costs low. The rehearsal dinner of simple food was at our house. My cousin Lavon is a chef and was breaking into the wedding cake business at the time and she made ours as a wedding present. Instead of serving cocktails, we served wine, beer, and soda for our guests. My friend Rachel acted as our coordinator for the day of the event. She delivered pay to the professionals who provided services and made decisions that needed to be addressed that day.

We initially thought that we would make the bouquets and boutonnieres ourselves the day before the wedding. Once I considered the time that would take, in addition to all the other last-minute tasks, it made sense to have a florist provide them. We compromised by gathering lilacs from my mother's garden for the altar and the tables. Rick was working with another carpenter who sidelined as a DJ, and he gave us a great deal. My favorite memory of the DJ and the dancing is when my parents, my brothers, and I were all out on the dance floor doing the Electric Slide. Now we just need to teach the dance to Rick.

During the planning process, my mother and her army of friends expected to cook for the wedding. Cooking to make an event special may well be a natural tendency for any Filipina. Unfortunately, the venue we chose allowed only caterers from a pre-determined list. If the managers there had tasted my mother's fine Filipino cuisine, they might have added her to their list. Instead, we compromised with my parents by asking them to host a party at our house the day after the wedding. This worked out beautifully. The sun was shining brightly for the party. We had a lot of out-of-town wedding guests to entertain, as well as people who my parents had wanted to invite to the wedding, but who didn't fit in our budget-conscious guest list. All of them and our entire guest list were invited to this party. As a result, we spent a lot more time with our guests. The event included a roasted pig, Filipino noodles called *pancit*, lumpia, and all the fixings for a grand celebration.

Other measures helped save a few dollars here and there. Hemming my wedding dress to the right length for me created a lot of leftover fabric. My mom's friend made the pillow for the ring bearer from that extra fabric. Our photographer happened to live in the neighborhood, so he and his wife stopped by the day after the wedding. Some of the photos he took that day are among my favorites.

When planning our honeymoon, we found a cruise to the Caribbean for an amazing deal. The Iraq war had just started, and this ship was being diverted from the Mediterranean. As a result of the savings, we were able to add a few days to our honeymoon and enjoy the amusement parks in Orlando.

Counting the ceremony, reception, and honeymoon, the grand total of our celebration was around $12,000. That's just about right for a do-it-yourself kind of guy and a financially savvy bride. We went slightly over our budget in certain areas and received some very generous gifts in others, but ultimately struck the right balance.

"THIS MAGIC MOMENT"

Our wedding day was magical. The details faded away in the joy and celebration. I don't know if I have ever smiled as big or as much in my life. The whole experience of getting dressed and ready—incorporating something borrowed and something blue, naturally—added to the drama. Watching my mom and matron of honor get their hair done while sitting next to me increased my excitement. Auntie Lydia, who felt that she was representing all of my mom's family from the Philippines, graciously paid for the salon visit. The expression on Rick's face when he first saw me walking down the stairs all decked out in my wedding dress is something that I will never forget.

My grandmother attended to make her toast, which has become a tradition in my dad's family. My grandpa used to do this toast, but he passed away when I was still a teenager. Grandma Betty still tears up as she recounts in her toast the fifty-plus years of marriage they shared together before he died. She says that the secret to their success was communication. "Communicate, communicate, communicate," she states emphatically. Then she always follows this with a line that everyone usually chuckles at and applauds. With a big smile, she says, "Never go to bed angry. Talk it out and then make love."

Not everything in our wedding went as planned. We had hoped for sunshine and practiced walking through the ceremony outside. But May weather is not something you can count on in western Washington. In the end, we had to move the ceremony inside and make a mad rush to a nearby store to purchase candles. Rick's nephew, the ring bearer, had a hard time finding his cute little smile. I am sure his tiny tuxedo felt uncomfortable. The beautiful bouquets were much larger than I had thought they would be. Still, the day was perfect.

The ceremony left me and many guests reaching for tissues to dab at our eyes. Having my oldest friend as my matron of honor and my new sisters-in-law as bridesmaids was very special. Matt was Rick's best man, and my two brothers were groomsmen. They were all so handsome in their tuxedos. My youngest brother, Ryan, played the trumpet for us as we walked down the aisle as husband and wife.

The rest of the busy evening involved reuniting with friends, chatting with family from out of town, and getting down on the dance floor. The food was delicious, the wine flowed, and the catering staff was invisible. My brother Loren surprised us with a rendition of one of our favorite Billy Joel songs, "Just the Way You Are." I truly believe that moments such as an exchange of vows should be celebrated. When two people find each other and pledge to spend the rest of their lives loving each other, toasts and other festivities are a must.

KEEPING PERSPECTIVE

Lately, it seems that some brides are going way over the top with their wedding day plans. A new term, *bridezilla*, succinctly describes these women. With so many marriages ending in divorce, you would think that they would be more mindful of what's really important about a wedding. The number of bridezillas also makes me wonder about the pressure brides feel to plan the perfect day. This tremendous pressure comes from society, magazines, and family members and friends who aggressively push their opinions about what a wedding day should be.

There is a big difference between a wedding and a marriage. Your wedding celebrates the day you and your new spouse start your life together. Your marriage is the rest of your life together. Both are important to consider. I believe it is critical to plan your wedding with your marriage in mind. What do you want your marriage to be like? If you spend every dollar you have, and some you don't, on this one day, you'll start your new life penniless or in debt. And if your parents want to help as you begin this new phase, maybe their help could be directed toward another meaningful gift, such as a down payment toward a home or home furnishings for your future together. I have seen some wedding budgets equal to what I spent on my first condo. If you have an unlimited budget, enjoy making the most of your wedding day. I would still encourage you to be intentional about what the day means for you and your soon-to-be spouse. How you orchestrate it could illustrate what your marriage means to you.

Rick and I talked extensively about what we would like our marriage to be. We looked at our parents' marriages and saw pieces that we wanted to encourage and some that we didn't. Since Rick had been married before, he had an even better idea of what he was looking for: a partnership. He prefers a relationship where both have a voice in the decision-making process. This wasn't the case with his parents. While his dad was out to sea, his mom had to rule the roost. She disciplined the kids, balanced the checkbook, and maintained the house. She earned the nickname "Sarge" because of how she managed the household. Rick's first marriage also taught him that the patterns you don't see can sneak up on you and create difficulties. I am so glad we waited until he was ready to marry. It takes even more courage to try again after the first time doesn't work out.

Sunday brunch

....

While planning for your wedding, discuss these questions with your spouse:

- Who will contribute financially to the cost of your wedding? If you let others contribute to the cost, consider that they may also want their voices heard as you make decisions about your wedding.

- What do you want to splurge on, and what are you willing to do without?

- Can you cut costs by enlisting the help of friends or family on do-it-yourself projects?

GETTING ORGANIZED

Fortunately, a lot of fantastic resources are available to help you with your wedding budget and planning. These include books with charts and checklists, and online sites that point out often-overlooked details. Try these stress-saving tips:

- Create your guest list with your budget in mind. The more people on your list, the higher your budget will need to be to feed and entertain them.

- Be aware of hidden costs like gratuities, taxes, and delivery fees. These can add up and wreak havoc on your budget.

- Carefully track actual spending and compare it to your spending plan.

9

HOME SWEET HOME

Throughout our engagement, and even long before it, the wish to find a new home for Rick and me was often on my mind. In fact, when I had first moved in with Rick, I'd begun talking to him about finding a home of our own. Rick purchased his house in 1986 with his first wife. It was a nice house with a two-car garage. It had three bedrooms, two bathrooms, a family room, and a generous backyard. My conundrum wasn't the size or layout; the place just didn't feel like our house. Rick said that I could decorate the house however I wanted. But using my money to decorate his house felt strange. If I had believed that it would fix how I felt about that house, we could have discussed this more, developed a budget, or found another way to make the house ours. We talked about remodeling it. We drew plans on graph paper to push the back walls out, expanding the kitchen, family room, and master bedroom. He even liked the idea of adding a second floor. But living in that house while remodeling did not sound fun to me. I've heard that a remodel seriously tests a relationship. Regardless, I wasn't sure that a remodel would change my feelings about the house.

Previously, Rick had thought he would live in that house for the rest of his life. It was the first home he had ever purchased. It was where he was raising his son. He had invested a lot of sweat equity into finishing the family room and customizing the home for his family's needs. His house was only a mile or two from his mom's place, which was the same house he had lived in through high school and college. Though, like me, Rick was a Navy brat, his reaction to all the moving around during his childhood was settling down with deep roots.

Still, once we became engaged, I hoped that Rick might be more amenable to the idea of our buying a new house together. I regularly surveyed my friends to see if I was being reasonable in wanting a fresh start in a new place. I would begin those conversations by asking something like, "How would you feel about moving into the house that your boyfriend bought with his former wife?" My friends generally responded by saying, "Wow, I don't know. Getting used to that would be hard. I'm not sure how I would feel exactly. I would probably feel more comfortable if we found a new place that was ours instead."

That's how I felt, too. It was a little strange when Rick's ex-wife came over to pick up Matt and seemed more comfortable in the home than I was. I was growing tired of looking at white walls, and I wanted to feel free to paint and decorate in a way that reflected both Rick's style and mine. Though he had given me permission to decorate as I liked, I felt that I needed his approval for each project since the house was his. I wanted both of us to work together to create our space. What's more, it seemed that my things were shoehorned into his house. I thought that we could combine our resources and find a house where we could both feel at home. I just needed to convince Rick.

By the time of our engagement, Rick and I had been having

the conversation about finding a new home for a couple of years. To be willing to give up his first home and move, he required that certain criteria be met. First, our new house had to fall within the boundaries of Matt's school district. Ideally, it would be within a few miles of Rick's current house. Second, it needed to have a real backyard instead of a postage-stamp size lot. Rick preferred a three-car garage, too, but didn't require it.

I was motivated to find a new home. Whenever I went for a walk in the neighborhood, I kept my eyes peeled for homes for sale. Occasionally, after a dinner out or on a Sunday afternoon, we would drive around and look for houses for sale, but that was just window shopping. Since our engagement, Rick had become more open to the idea of moving, but wasn't ready to act on it.

This was during the early 2000s, a time when new houses were appearing everywhere. Developers turned farmland and vacant lots into subdivisions and townhomes. Home values were healthy. It would be several years before houses would become overpriced and the real estate bubble would burst.

A POSTCARD-PERFECT HOME

One day, I came home from work to find a postcard on the kitchen counter. The postcard depicted a two-story house, which was labeled "just listed." Rick had collected the mail and set this postcard aside for me. He asked if I recognized the house. It took me a moment to recall that it was in a cul-de-sac just a couple of blocks away in a neighborhood I walked through regularly.

Many of Rick's former neighbors had moved into this cul-de-sac of upgraded homes when it had been built. Rick had sometimes wished that he'd moved into this neighborhood then. We talked to these neighbors when they walked their dogs or when their kids sold candy for school fundraisers. Matt had grown up and played with several kids on that street. He'd participated in T-ball and Little League with one of the boys. A bunch of them would catch lizards and frogs in the pond around the corner from that cul-de-sac. Near the pond, they would play in a tree they dubbed the Swing Tree because of the swing someone had put up. The people on this street were the type who got together for Fourth of July barbecues and went all out for Christmas decorations. The house on the postcard was the first one to go up for sale in that cul-de-sac in the eight years since its development.

I realized that by setting out the postcard for me to see, Rick was telling me that he was open to the idea of looking at this house. We walked down the street and into the cul-de-sac for a closer view. On the way, Rick pointed out the homes of folks he knew because their kids had grown up with Matt. He tried to explain to me who had lived where on our street before they moved to this street. I tried to listen, but was distracted by the possibility that we could be looking at our new house.

The outside of the house had interesting architectural details that appealed to Rick. The hipped roof and gables added a lot of charm to the roofline. The yard seemed well maintained and included a row of boxwoods that highlighted a Japanese maple. The home had only a two-car garage, but the driveway was long and provided room for the excessive number of cars Rick owned. These included a work van, his truck, and his 1968 Pontiac GTO. He also needed garage space for a workbench and tools. As a finish carpenter, he has a lot of tools.

Walking home, I could barely contain my excitement about the house and Rick's willingness to take the home-buying idea one step further. Curiosity and the hope of new possibilities led us to call a friend who was a real estate agent to schedule a full tour. By the next day, we were touring the inside of the house. From the moment we walked in, we could easily see ourselves building a life together there. The family room, eating area, and kitchen were all in a large, shared space with hardwood floors and Berber carpet. The master bedroom was pleasantly large, with a wonderful soaking tub, a walk-in closet, and double sinks. There were two other bedrooms, one for Matt and one where his band could practice. The house had a large backyard instead of the small lots you see so often these days. We thought it would be a nice upgrade from where we were living.

We discussed the possibilities of that house over the next day or two and asked if we could walk through one more time. The first time we saw it I had been very excited, and I'd since forgotten some of the details. The owners agreed but because it was Halloween, they asked if they could stay so they could feed their kids before trick-or-treating. When we arrived, we saw their three children in costume eating Tater Tot Casserole. We chatted a little about the builder upgrades that they chose and the neighborhood. After another quick tour, we said goodbye and walked home while chatting excitedly about what to do next.

THE OFFER AND INSPECTION

After that visit and discussions with our agent, we decided to make an offer. That was the exciting part. What followed was the usual back-and-forth, negotiating this and that. Inspections, further negotiations, and compromises occupied our evenings. Generally, after the initial offer, the home-buying process gets more difficult. Our agent was a huge help in enabling us to buy this home for the right price and ensuring that all the aspects of what we were buying were disclosed to us.

After our initial inspection, we learned that the siding on our house was a type that could easily fail if not maintained properly. In fact, half of the siding was failing or would do so soon. We brought out a siding expert to give us an estimate of what the cost would be to repair or replace it.

Other little issues that we hadn't previously noticed surfaced in the inspection. The vinyl flooring in the laundry room was torn. All the bathrooms were missing toilet paper holders and some lacked towel holders. These weren't major concerns, but they were a part of our negotiations. We took each step knowing that this was the right house, but still, this part of the process lasted weeks. Once the deal was mutually agreed upon, the time came to sell Rick's house.

At this time, we knew that we qualified for the new house, but we still needed to finalize some decisions: What selling price would be reasonable for Rick's house? Should we also sell the condo or keep renting it? The condo had a tenant whose lease wasn't up until the middle of the following year. If we sold just his house and kept the condo, exactly what would our mortgage payments be? We decided to keep the condo as an investment and defer the decision to sell it until after the tenant's lease ended. After considering what homes were selling for in the neighborhood and upgrades that Rick had made, we agreed on a listing price with the real estate agent.

MAGIC IN THE DETAILS

Rick and I went to work as usual on the Monday that his house was listed. We had not had a chance to coach Matt on what to do when someone wanted to see the house. Sometime that afternoon, after Matt had arrived home from school, an agent called to ask permission to show it. Matt took the call and let the agent know that it was okay to come over.

When showing your home, you are expected to vacate it for an hour or so. This allows the potential buyers to feel comfortable as they look around, peek into closets and cabinets, and consider if this house meets their needs. Instead, Matt took the agent and buyers for a complete tour of the house. He showed them the custom cabinets Rick had made for the family room and most of the closets. He played his drums for them. He showed them the swing set in the backyard and some of the stunts that he can do from it. He did these things with all the charm of a fourteen-year-old boy.

Imagine our surprise when we learned later that afternoon that these buyers wanted to make an offer on our home. The buyers were a young couple looking for a home where they could start a family. The husband also played the drums. The wife was an elementary school teacher in the school district. They loved the backyard and the potential it offered. Our agent, their agent, Rick, and I all met a few hours later to go over the conditions of the offer. They were able to meet most of our conditions, and by the end of the evening, the offer had been mutually accepted all around—on the same day it had been listed. It all happened incredibly fast thanks to the miracles of technology and the buyers' level of commitment. It was a very easy process, especially compared with what we went through with the owners of the house we were buying. In that situation, each offer and counteroffer had taken a day or two.

We have always felt that whole experience hinted of magic. We didn't go out shopping with the real estate agent for homes; the postcard was delivered to us. The young buyers of our house had been looking for one just like it for several months. They had made offers on a couple of other homes, but for one reason or another, the deals kept falling through. The husband was also in the trades, like Rick, and played the drums, like Matt. His first name and his wife's were the same as those of Rick's brother-in-law and youngest sister.

The uncanny details didn't end there. The number twenty-three has always been special to me. The twenty-third is the date I was born, the date my mother was born, the date Rick and I first went out, and the date of many other extraordinary events that I won't recount here. The buyers' earnest money check was dated October 23rd, as was the postmark on the "just listed" postcard. Then the closing date was Rick's birthday. We felt that all this was confirmation that we were doing the right thing. Our agent even accused me of sacrificing a goat to create this miracle.

This all felt magical, but was it really? It seemed a miracle that Rick was interested in this house. In reality, he was open to the idea of buying a home together because we had gotten engaged. Our wedding was set for May of the next year. He'd asked me to marry him because he'd decided to spend the rest of his life with me. He hadn't made that decision or commitment when we were just living together. It made sense that he hadn't been ready to buy a house together until he knew that he wanted to marry me.

How well it all worked out showed us that the time and place were right to buy our new home. We felt that the people who bought Rick's home would love and cherish it as much as he did. We drive by that house almost every day. And the house we live in now is as much a part of our love story as our wedding day.

WHEN THE TIMING ISN'T RIGHT

A couple of years ago, my friend Rachel moved into her partner's house after they had been together for a while. Their future plans included moving farther north and buying a home that represented both of them and that was closer to Rachel's parents. Her partner, Tammy, owned her home, and unfortunately, by the time they felt ready to find a new one, housing prices had declined substantially. The housing bubble had burst. Their neighborhood had an excess inventory of homes for sale. Their house remained on the market for several months without a serious buyer.

The timing isn't always right to move to a new home. Factors outside your control can hinder you. Now, Rachel and Tammy are biding their time until more buyers in their area are in the market for a home like theirs. Meanwhile, they are making small improvements to increase the marketability and value of their current home so they will have more money from the sale to put toward their new home.

To take advantage of good timing when it does arrive, be prepared: Have a plan or a dream, be open to possibilities, and gather the resources you need to act. One element of being in the right place at the right time is looking for that moment and feeling ready for it. Otherwise the opportunity becomes lost in the background, or in the junk mail in our case.

Sunday brunch

Consider these tips and suggestions from Rick:

- Being sensitive to the needs of your partner is helpful. It didn't bother Rick that we were living in his house. But he later felt that since it bothered me so much, it should have mattered to him too. Are you being sensitive to the needs of your partner? Are you thinking about yourself, or about the both of you?

- As an interesting exercise with your partner, list your top five financial goals and priorities for the next few years while your spouse lists his or hers. Then list what you think your partner's top five priorities are, and have your partner try to identify yours. Compare the two sets of lists. How well do they match up?

- Buying a house costs a lot of money and is a big decision. Take time to consider your options. Make a list of pros and cons to assure your rational mind. Then listen to your gut and trust your instincts.

10

TO MERGE OR NOT
TO MERGE

Probably one of the most controversial topics that I talk about with my friends is whether to merge checking accounts with a spouse's. It certainly stirred up controversy between Rick and me. This subject can be as thorny as the debate over whether a woman should change her last name to her husband's or whether to have children. As time goes on, men's and women's roles continue to evolve, and these decisions, financial and otherwise, are not automatic as they once were. You don't have to do things the way they have always been done. In fact, because there are so many choices available, it has become even harder to decide what to do.

About six months after we married, Rick suggested that we merge our checking accounts. At the time, we each had our own accounts, though we maintained a joint account for household expenses, including food. We individually contributed a percentage of our income from every paycheck to the joint account.

To say that I was surprised by his proposal to merge accounts is a gross understatement. Just a year or two earlier, before we were engaged but while we were living together, Rick had brought up the subject of a prenuptial agreement. When he went through his divorce, things changed for him financially. He refinanced his house to cash out his ex-wife and started paying child support. He became solely responsible for a larger mortgage payment. He now had to play a larger role in the upkeep of himself and his son.

By starting the discussion about a prenuptial agreement, Rick was trying to make sure that what was his stayed his, and that his interests and his son's were protected. At that time, I didn't know anyone else with a prenuptial agreement, other than celebrities in tabloids or rich people with old money. My friends never talked about these agreements. I understood that Rick didn't want to start over again financially if our relationship failed. I understood that he wanted to protect himself and his son. I didn't understand how a prenuptial agreement was appropriate in our situation.

At the time, we both owned our own homes. My condo wasn't valued as highly as his house, but it was providing a little rental income. Our jobs paid in the same range, although Rick was making slightly more than I was. We both owned our vehicles free and clear. I had been saving into a 401(k) plan for years, and he had his pension. We had different methods for saving, but essentially, we were both savers by nature. He had more savings than I did, and I still carried a little leftover debt. Since Rick is thirteen years older than I am, he'd had more time to establish himself financially. Being younger, I was still getting started, but was well on my way to a strong financial foundation.

The discussion about creating a prenuptial agreement was heated. I can't remember exactly what was said, and neither can Rick, except for one part: I remember telling him that I couldn't begin with the end in mind. I felt that our assets were similar, so I didn't understand the need for a prenup. I said that I would write: "I don't want your damn house, I don't want your damn truck, and I don't want your damn money. All I want is you." I don't remember how the conversation started or ended, only that part. I remember tears and yelling and being completely taken aback.

Of course, I knew why he'd brought the subject up: He was scared. He was scared of repeating mistakes. He was scared of our marriage possibly ending the same way that his last one had. And he was scared of the future and of all the unknowns.

A few days later, we were able to have this discussion in a more rational tone. Rick felt more comfortable when he learned that in the state of Washington, property and assets that you possess before your marriage remain your separate property after a divorce. Also, other than the equity in his home, we simply didn't have significant differences in our respective incomes and assets. In the end, we decided we didn't need a prenuptial agreement.

When the differences in income and assets are significant, it is more appropriate to have a prenup. This is especially true for older couples, second marriages, and blended families. All parties should make sure that they are taking care of themselves and any children who are their responsibility. Although a prenuptial agreement can make you feel that you are planning the end of your marriage before it begins, it may be the responsible thing to do to protect yourself. Those who are planning to marry must fully disclose their finances, hopes, and fears to one another before they tie the knot. Unfortunately, the reality is that today, many marriages end in divorce.

ABOUT-FACE

Fast-forward to the day when Rick suggested that we merge our checking accounts, a few years later. This was six months into our newlywed life, but he told me that he couldn't feel that we were truly married until we merged our accounts. I was surprised not just at the topic, but also at the timing. For almost a year, we had been living in our new house that we had purchased together. I let him know that his suggestion surprised me, given our discussion about a prenuptial agreement a couple of years before. I had thought we would continue to operate the way that we had been for the remainder of our marriage. He said he had thought about it and discussed it with a friend. He felt that now was the right time to merge our checking accounts. He said he understood that I was surprised, but that he felt strongly about this.

I considered how merging accounts would affect our handling of finances in the future. I enjoyed our existing system. Our individual contributions to the joint account were based partially on our income and partially on the number of people who were our responsibility. I was making a little less than Rick was, and we also needed to account for Matt. Teenage boys take up a lot of space and eat a lot of food. We each took care of our individual expenses and responsibilities; then we paid the bills for the house out of our joint account.

I realized that the biggest change would involve being more accountable to each other for our expenditures. Apparently for Rick this was not a big deal. He had been married before and had shared a checking account and financial responsibilities. I had not had these experiences. So the obstacles in merging our accounts, which I had thought were his, were actually mine. My money had always been my money. I was used to saving or spending it however I wished. Although I was generally a responsible citizen and had a credit score that reflected this, I was accountable to no one except myself.

What really scared me was how merging accounts might change our relationship. I feared that this could put me into a submissive position where he was the boss and I would have to report to him on how I spent my money. As a modern, enlightened woman, I would not live that way. Later in that conversation, I let him know that if I wanted to have a facial, I would. If I saw a pair of shoes that I had

In 2010, research firm Harris Interactive conducted a poll showing that 31 percent of Americans who had merged their finances had lied to their partners about money. Of those who lied, 58 percent hid cash and 54 percent concealed minor purchases.

to have, I would buy them. I was not going to let him turn me into my mother. As I said that out loud, it struck me as a revelation. A previous conversation with my mom came to mind, and I shared it with Rick.

She had said, "I found a few plants on clearance today at the store. They were almost dead, so I got a really good deal on them, just a dollar each. You can have some of them if you want. I will bring them back to life and when they are healthier, I will give some to you. Just don't tell your dad."

"Why can't I tell Dad?" I had asked. She'd replied, "I told him that my friend gave them to me."

My mother is a wonderful person, and I absolutely love her. She has always wanted the best for me, whether I wanted to grow up to be a doctor or Miss America. Unfortunately, she has been caught amid shifting feelings about women working outside the home, cultural differences, and changing generational attitudes. From years of observing my parents, I can guess a couple of the reasons why she felt she couldn't tell my dad that she bought those plants.

Although Mom babysat when I was younger, sold crafts or food at bazaars, and worked outside the home for a few years to pay off our braces, these were things she did for extra money, vacations, or funds to send back home to the Philippines. My dad was the breadwinner. Mom took care of us, the house, and all our friends.

While I was growing up, Dad seemed to think about money often, whether it was to find a way to buy a piece of property, invent the latest and greatest gadget, or balance the checkbook. Sometimes there was debt to pay down or college to save for. I remember him explaining the things he was thinking about to my mother, but the finances didn't weigh on her mind the same way they did on my dad's.

I don't know if my dad told her not to spend any more money, or if he told her that they didn't need any more plants in their house. I do know that it would have taken only a slightly critical tone in my dad's voice to make my mom feel defensive. She would return to him a disapproving look. Then her response to keep purchases a secret would be reinforced. This story is insignificant enough in their lives that they don't remember it, but I knew that I didn't want to follow the same pattern.

After recounting this to Rick, I told him, "I don't want to lie to you." Then he said the most magical words to me: "Sweetheart, I trust your judgment." Wow! That meant the world to me.

Until we had this conversation, I was not aware that I had issues to work through regarding money, control, power, freedom, and independence. I didn't realize how fearful I was of losing authority over my income. I did not want Rick telling me what I could and could not do. Keeping my own accounts was my way of retaining control and independence.

Looking back, I can see how some of my feelings could have been because of our age difference. Especially at the start of our relationship, I would defer to Rick on big decisions. Since he was older, I thought he knew more about some things. Sometimes I felt I had to justify my decisions to him. I was trying to impress upon him somehow that, really, I was a grown-up. Rick had astonished me by saying that he trusted my judgment. As a result of this discussion, I was able to see that we could merge our checking accounts and that it wouldn't be the end of the world or my financial freedom. He obviously respected me and my decision-making abilities. I felt responsible to maintain the trust that he had placed in me.

These two conversations—one about prenuptial agreements and the other about merging our checking accounts—illustrate that neither of us had the skills to effectively introduce a radical, new subject or the ability to rationally discuss it. We have learned that it can take us several days to work through a weighty subject. Our typical intro is, "Is this a good time to talk about money?" During the conversation, I will likely have an emotional outburst. Rick will probably grow quiet. We will need to step away from each other and come back with love and respect as the foundation for our conversation.

TEAM EFFORT

After our lengthy discussion of whether to merge accounts, we consolidated and closed a few accounts and added each other as joint owner to the savings accounts that we kept. Now I agree with Rick that completely merging our accounts helps us feel fully married. We share the financial burdens of mortgages, car payments, and household bills. We don't have to tell each other every little thing we buy each day. Still, we have an obligation to each other to be honest about where our hard-earned money goes.

Our main accounts landed at my credit union. Because I had

been a member there since 1995, it made sense to add Rick as a joint owner on everything instead of starting a new account. This has been a slight inconvenience for him. I am the primary account holder, so there are a few things that he cannot access without my permission.

Then there are the daily logistics of maintaining a joint checking account. Rick has a bill-paying system that works for him. As he processes the mail, he notes on the outside of the envelope when the bill is due. All the bills go in a pile on his desk. He thumbs through it every few days and makes sure he is up to date. Until a few years ago, he still liked to pay bills with checks and then balance his checkbook. When we opened the checking account at my credit union, it had a much better online bill-paying system that I encouraged him to try.

If your way of paying bills works for you, keep it up. Rick thought his method of sending checks and balancing the checkbook worked, but it didn't. He didn't like balancing his checkbook, so he would amass two or three months' worth of statements to review. He would sit in the family room with his head bent over a calculator, agonizing over any errors in his checkbook. They were usually simple math errors he had made as he hurriedly scrawled notes in the register. Figuring it all out would sometimes take an hour or two. During that time, I was invisible. He was laser-focused on those statements in front of him. He was so focused that I could dance naked in front of him and he might say, "That's nice," if he noticed at all.

He tried the online bill paying and likes it more than it irritates him. He originally thought he had to give up control over when he paid his bills, but he realized that he could determine when money left our checking account. Now, whenever he is working on something and becomes oblivious to his surroundings, I tease,

"Are you balancing your checkbook?" This is my playful way of letting him know that he isn't paying attention to anything else. If that is his intention, I know to give him a little space so he can work through his project.

I keep an eye on our longer-term finances to balance out our financial responsibilities. I enjoy working with our investments; Rick doesn't, and he has little experience investing. You can't merge your retirement accounts because they are associated with your individual Social Security numbers, but I still track all of them. Even when you define individual areas of responsibility, it is important to know what is happening with your partner's areas. I share news about our investments, how much we can contribute to our retirement accounts and changes we are making. Rick is comforted by having these investments and understands how they are doing. I appreciate that he takes care of the daily details of banking and bill paying.

Working with your finances isn't all about numbers and math. It is also about prioritizing and decision making. Having a certain level of organization can help ensure that bills are paid on time. Sometimes people who think they are bad at math also think they are bad with money. The two traits don't always coincide. Calculators, spreadsheets, and online tools can help offset a lack of math skills. Then you can strengthen your prioritizing, decision-making, and organizing skills.

WHAT WORKS FOR US

Rick and I have unwritten rules for spending that we both seem to follow instinctually. Our significant number seems to be around a hundred dollars. When either of us is purchasing new clothing, household goods, or car accessories, we discuss most purchases exceeding that number. In the past, I have come home to find a new receiver hooked up to our television or a box at our doorstep with a new part for his car or truck. In most cases, we had already discussed the purchase of these items and he finally got up the nerve to spend the money.

Before I met Rick, I rarely kept any money separate from my checking or savings account. But I've since adopted his special treatment for money from out-of-the-ordinary sources, such as a bonus, a side job, a birthday check, or a Christmas gift. When Rick receives a check from his mom for his birthday, for example, he promptly cashes it and puts the money in a certain place to save it for something special. We usually apply bonuses or the occasional financial Christmas gift toward a special purchase for us or for the house. This is how we finally purchased our last couch and completed the tile backsplash in our kitchen.

DETERMINING WHAT WORKS FOR YOU

I used to manage a credit union branch and observed couples who never merged their accounts. This seemed to lead to secrecy within their marriage. If you were to poll financial advisors or family law attorneys, many of them would advise keeping accounts separate. However, if you polled marriage counselors, they would likely disagree with that advice. True, sharing an account can make it tricky to surprise your partner with a birthday, anniversary, or Christmas gift. But with a little creativity, you can succeed.

Still, there are good reasons not to merge accounts. One or both of you may have a financial obstacle to overcome first—for example, significant credit card debt or student loan balances, spousal support, or credit issues. If you are unsure which avenue suits you best, consult the experts. Attorneys, financial advisors, ministers, and counselors may be able to help you determine questions to ask yourself and your partner when considering this choice. Even if you and your partner decide not to share your money, regular conversations about your finances are helpful.

Sunday brunch

- What are the differences, financial and otherwise, between being roommates and being married?

- Is it appropriate for you two to merge your accounts?

- What must you let go of to merge finances harmoniously? (Think: stereotypes, hang-ups, habits.)

- If you don't merge your accounts, what additional actions must you take to stay on the same page financially?

- What are some potential pitfalls you can think of now so you can avoid them in the future?

11

STEPMONSTER

Have you seen the movie *Stepmom* with Susan Sarandon, Ed Harris, and Julia Roberts? In it, Julia Roberts plays a woman who becomes the stepmother of a young boy and a teenage girl. In one scene she jokes, "Can we cover up my evil stepmother wart, 'cause it must be showing." This and other stereotypes about stepmothers live on in our society: Consider Cinderella's stepmother or the evil witch in Disney's *Snow White*. Is that really how children feel about their stepparents? I know that every blended family is a little different. In the end, we are just trying to do our best for the kids. Every time I watch *Stepmom*, I still cry when Julia Roberts is asked to be a part of the family picture at Christmas.

Early in our relationship, Rick and I had the discussion about kids. Rick had decided he didn't want more kids. He didn't want to be old when they graduated from high school. Before that first discussion about children, I had always assumed that I would become a mother. I didn't think much about making that choice. I assumed that getting married, having kids, and being a mother was just what women did. When I learned that Rick didn't want more children, I had to seriously evaluate what I wanted. I deliberated for months. If I wanted kids, Rick was not the man for me.

During those months of deliberation, I was trying to figure out if having children was truly my desire, or if I was responding to familial and cultural ideas of what I should want. I am the only daughter in my family and the oldest, so I felt that it was my responsibility to provide grandkids for my parents. I wasn't the only one who felt that I should. My mother was always asking when I was going to start having kids. The thought would creep in at random times: "Do I or don't I want children?" While shopping, I would walk by the baby department and touch the clothes and blankets. I had friends with children and I would look for that twinge, that maternal urge that I hear them talk about.

What I learned after much research, heartfelt conversation, and soul searching is that I didn't want children. I told Rick that I was 90 percent sure I didn't want them. I was still young, only twenty-six, when I made this decision. I was comfortable with my decision at the time, but I wasn't sure what feelings the next ten to fifteen years would bring. So I reserved the right to change my mind. I shared with Rick that when I walked by the baby department and saw an adorable outfit, my thought was, "Who else could I buy this for?" When I saw parents with their kids, the twinge I felt was not heartache or loss; it was mostly irritation at the noise. When I listened to my heart, it said, "You have already done this."

My youngest brother, Ryan, is eleven years younger than I am. I changed his diapers, fed him, put him to sleep, and played with him. I realized that when I thought about having children I felt that I had already been there, done that. Ryan has grown up and we enjoy a close relationship, but we still struggle sometimes with my role as a big sister who moonlights as a second mom.

It was freeing to say out loud to Rick that I didn't want kids. Now, I can completely enjoy holding a baby or playing with a cousin or nephew without feeling the need to analyze. I have also learned that I still love children; I just don't feel the need to create one of my own.

A WHOLE NEW BALL GAME

By the time Rick and I got married, I had been a part of Matt's life for two and a half years. He was fifteen years old when he was the best man in our wedding. As an only child, he was used to doing things his way. For example, as the date of our wedding approached, Rick suggested that Matt get a haircut. Matt somehow never got around to it until a couple of weeks after the wedding. So all our wedding pictures show him with a long, shaggy, curly head of hair instead of the cleaned-up look he wore later.

After Rick's divorce, Matt spent half of his time with his dad and half with his mom, who lived nearby. I understood that I was not his mom, so I didn't even try to be. When he would do something that I disapproved of, I consciously thought about whether it was the type of behavior that was appropriate for me to correct, or if it was something his dad should do. In age, I am halfway between Rick and Matt. Rick is thirteen years older than I am, and I am thirteen years older than Matt. This gave me a different perspective on things that I would share with Matt regarding school, friends, and girls. I tried to share those ideas as a concerned adult instead of as a parent or buddy.

Early in our relationship, when Matt was twelve, he was very clear that he did not like me hanging around. When I came over for dinner, he would be sullen and difficult to talk with. Sometimes I would show up and he would say, "What's she doing here again?" When it was time for him to go to bed, he would try to get me to leave by yelling, "I am not going to sleep until she leaves!" If I tried to leave, Rick asked me to stay. I thought most kids had grown out of throwing temper tantrums by age twelve. Matt had not.

Matt was involved in Little League, and I looked forward to attending those games even though they could be uncomfortable. Matt played first base, or sometimes he would pitch. He was a decent player, but had high expectations of his performance and would get frustrated when things didn't turn out the way he wanted. Still, it was fun and exciting to cheer on those twelve- and thirteen-year-old boys.

Attending those games was completely out of the ordinary for me. They were an escape, a great reason to keep my workday to a reasonable schedule instead of the pace and length I had been maintaining. I got to know Rick's ex-wife a little, meet his neighbors, and know some of Matt's friends. The whole experience was enlightening: This was how suburban families spent their time, as opposed to how my single friends and I did.

No matter how loud I cheered at those Little League games, Matt was still not a fan of me. I was the home-electronics manager at a large retail store and felt that I was hip to what music kids liked. I brought over a newly released Foo Fighters CD for him to hear. I thought that music could be a bridge between all our ages. Those attempts did not ingratiate me as easily as I had hoped they would. What we really needed was time.

Over the next few years, Matt and I started getting along better. He could tell that I wasn't going anywhere, and I tried to be patient. One weekend while we were all camping with his grandmother, Matt and I were at the family center playing pool. He was winning, but I was still trying. We were laughing and teasing each other. Out of the blue, he stopped and apologized for acting how he had when he was younger. I really appreciated it and told him so. I tried not to get all teary-eyed. We went back to playing pool as if nothing had happened, but something had.

This would not be the end of my struggles as a stepmother, but I certainly felt that it was a step in the right direction. I think Matt could see that his dad loved and supported me, and that it didn't diminish Rick's love for Matt. I did appreciate Matt's reaching out. It was spontaneous and heartfelt, quite an accomplishment for a fourteen-year-old only child.

A PLACE ON THE FAMILY TREE

During Matt's first year of high school, he took a Spanish class. One of the projects that the teacher had the students work on was a family tree. On a large sheet of poster board, they were supposed to diagram their family as far back as they could and name each family member, along with the Spanish word for each relation. All three of us were in the family room while Matt was working on this. I glanced over at his work, and I didn't see a place for me on his family tree. I waited to see how the project would evolve. I glanced over occasionally to observe what he did next. He started coloring in the tree, and I still wasn't listed. Fighting back tears, I grabbed a book and headed upstairs to our bedroom.

I felt hurt and left out. Matt's behavior seemed inconsistent. He had been an excited participant in our wedding. He seemed happy in the new house. I thought we were a family. Later, Rick came upstairs to see what I was doing. He could tell by my eyes and the pile of tissues around the trash bin that I had been crying and asked what was wrong. I told him what I saw when Matt was working on his project and shared how I felt. He felt pretty certain that he had seen my name on the family tree. He went back downstairs to see and check on Matt's progress. When he returned, he told me that I was indeed there on the tree. Next to "Rick, *Padre*" was "Stacy, *Madrastra*," meaning "stepmother." Matt had added it after I went upstairs.

This experience ended well, but it would not be the last time I felt excluded. One event in particular comes to mind. When Matt started driving, his mom bought an old pickup truck for them to share. She used it when she needed to haul stuff around. He used it as a daily driver for the most part. But then gas prices started creeping up. Matt's band practiced in the south part of Seattle. We lived in the suburbs fifteen miles north of the city. So Matt presented the idea that he should drive a little car with better mileage to reduce his fuel usage.

Rick and Matt scoured ads, test-drove a number of cars, and had a mechanic friend check things out under the hood. They finally decided on a Volkswagen Jetta. Rick was pleased that it wasn't a souped-up version. Matt was happy because it was a little sportier than the basic Jetta and it was black.

While they were shopping and test-driving, Rick and I talked often about if and how we could help Matt with this major purchase. I thought it would be helpful if Matt had the practice of writing a check every month. He already had a checking account. I didn't care if he wrote the check for insurance or a car payment, or if he wrote it to us—it was the habit that would be helpful, I thought. I also felt that we could help with the purchase, but I thought Matt should contribute some of his savings toward it. Rick and I seemed to have the same basic understanding.

Matt's mom was willing to put the proceeds of the truck sale toward the purchase of a new car. The items up for discussion were how much Matt should contribute and who was going to pay for his insurance and gas going forward.

At this time, Matt said, "It would be helpful if we could get together and discuss how to help me with the car." I thought, "That sounds great. Rick, his ex-wife, and I can all agree upon how we will help Matt." A date was set. Then I learned that "we" meant Matt, his mom, and Rick. I was not invited to be a part of the discussion. I was quietly furious. This was our money they were talking about—not just Rick's, ours. I could have made a stink and insisted on being there, could have fully stepped into my role as the evil stepmonster. But I didn't feel that was the right thing to do. Instead, I spent the afternoon pruning the heck out of our vine maple tree while they had this discussion around our kitchen table. My only comfort was the fact that Rick and I were on the same page about how we were willing to help Matt.

However, Rick caved. What dad doesn't want to give his son everything? Rick wanted to make buying the car easier for Matt. So in the end, Matt didn't contribute any of his savings toward it. We split the ongoing cost of his car insurance with his mom. Matt got everything he wanted. I had thought I would have a say in this decision, but I didn't.

In the future, decisions or discussions like that will never happen again without me there. Rick and I have agreed that we won't spend that amount of money without the full permission of the other person. Rick understands this and regrets that things unfolded the way they did. Such experiences illustrate a lesson for all participants. It would be so much easier if these lessons weren't such emotional minefields. You can understand where the danger might lie, but until you step on the mine, you don't see how great the impact is.

CUTTING THE APRON STRINGS

A couple of years later, Matt, Rick, and I were out for dinner at our favorite steak restaurant. At dinner, Matt shared with us that he thought he was ready to move out on his own. He had graduated from high school a few months earlier, so this conversation wasn't a big surprise. He felt that he was ready to support himself and have all his stuff in one place. Rick and I started asking questions about his income, expenses, and potential roommates. Matt felt that it would all work out fine, even though he had not completely thought through his expenses versus his income. We pointed out costs that he might not have considered: groceries, utilities, Internet and cell phone service, and car insurance.

We had been splitting Matt's cell phone and car insurance bill with his mom. Matt thought that we would continue to pay those for him. Rick informed him that if he moved out, we would expect him to be independent and to take care of those expenses. Matt was flabbergasted that we would cut him off completely.

I was thankful that Rick and I were on the same page without our having to discuss it ahead of time. We gently let Matt know that we were not cutting him off, but rather giving him the opportunity to be on his own. I can see how he might have thought that we would keep paying for those expenses. After all, we maintained paying child support until he moved out. That just felt like the right thing to do, given that his mom was on her own and that eighteen-year-old boys tend to eat a lot. We explained that if he needed help, we would always be there for him. And we have been there. Since that time, we have had numerous opportunities to support Matt, financially and in other ways. Between buying tools and tires for him, attending his shows, and letting his band practice at our house, we have demonstrated our support. We were even thanked in the liner notes of his band's latest CD release.

I learned early in our relationship that Rick generally operates assuming that everything will be the way it has always been. He took it as a given that Matt would go to college, as both Rick and Matt's mother had. Even with that mind-set, Rick didn't set aside much money specifically for Matt's schooling. He thought that on his salary he could afford Matt's tuition at the University of Washington, as long as expenses didn't increase. Whatever other requirements or desires Matt had—for example, room and board or the wish to go to another school—Rick expected to deal with as they arose. This goes against Rick's practical nature, but it does fit in with his ability to procrastinate. He is also uncomfortable doing anything new. So although he set aside some money in a savings account, it was insignificant compared with the cost of college. To save for college in a more meaningful way, Rick would have had to investigate college savings plans, like 529 plans, prepaid tuition plans, or other investment vehicles.

When I entered the picture, Rick's financial situation changed: We moved into a bigger house, Rick's steady employer of fifteen years laid him off, and I switched jobs. At the time, I didn't know about the need to set up a college fund for Matt. Being the planner in the family, I sarcastically thought that I should have thought of that.

A college fund ultimately proved unnecessary. At first Matt didn't go to college because he was in a hurry to move out and start working. He thought he would take a year off and then go. After being on his own for a little while, he moved back in with his mom for a period of time. Since he was already living at home, he decided to try school and had grand plans to earn a doctorate in music. He enrolled in one class and realized again that school was not his bag right then. Now he is working and focusing on his music with his band.

A few months ago, Rick came to me and said that Matt wanted to see if we could help him buy a newer truck. My instant gut reaction was unease that we would be opening an old wound. Rick then said, "This isn't going to be like last time." He laid out what he thought we could do. Matt needed $1,200, so we would give him six hundred and his mom would give him the same amount. Matt would pay us $50 a month over the course of a year, and make the same payments to his mom. I agreed to Rick's plan because it was reasonable and affordable, and because it distributed the responsibility. As Rick had promised, this time was completely different, and I appreciated his effort to make sure that it was.

> In 2005, Leflein Associates, a research company, asked five hundred teenagers ages thirteen to eighteen, "Do you believe the basics of money management should be a requirement in high school?" A staggering 80 percent of the teenagers polled said yes. Only 19 percent said no.

ALL GROWN UP

I have talked to a lot of people about the subjects of being a stepparent and blending families. I wonder if things would have been different if Matt had been a girl, or if he had been younger when we were introduced. Could Rick or I have acted differently to create a smoother transition? When he and I started dating, I didn't have friends with teenagers. Now, more of my friends are experiencing situations similar to mine. I think that all anyone can do is try to act in the best interests of their marriage and the children involved.

While Matt was growing up, I always hoped that once he became an adult, we would be able to relate to each other. I feel very fortunate that this has become our reality. We enjoy spending time together, and any old resentment seems to have faded.

Today, Matt is a self-sustaining, mature young man. He lives on his own and has a good job. He plays the drums with a band that performs up and down the West Coast. At some point in the future, he would like to get into a trade, as his father did. But with the downturn in the housing market and economy, he has had to put off those plans for a little while.

In the winter of 2009, several of us went on a short road trip over the mountains to check out Rick's and my new property in eastern Washington. Matt was driving because it was snowing and he had four-wheel drive. On the way there, he turned to me for advice about buying a house. He had been living in apartments or houses with roommates and was feeling the need for a place of his own. Ideally, he would be able to play his drums at concert volumes in this home. We chatted about credit scores, down payments, mortgages, and the responsibility of homeownership. I gave him the contact information for a friend of mine who is in the mortgage business. I had been about Matt's age when I prepared to buy my first home, and I was flattered that he felt comfortable talking about his finances with me and valued my advice.

A year later, Matt felt that he was ready to start looking for a house of his own. The timing was good for a first-time home buyer. Interest rates were low, and there was an abundance of homes on the market with motivated sellers. He had saved some money and had already talked to a mortgage lender about what loans he could qualify for. Matt was looking for a three-bedroom house with a yard. Space was important so he could have room to play his drums and still have a roommate if he wanted. He was used to living in the suburbs, so he didn't mind having to commute. He wasn't sure what he would find in his price range, but he was eager to discover a house with some possibilities.

Excitedly, I talked to Rick about helping Matt. To me, this

seemed like a great opportunity. It felt so different from when Matt was buying that first car. This house was an investment in his future, a way for him to further establish himself as an adult. Matt had proved to me that he could be responsible most of the time. If we could help him get into a house, I wanted to do so.

Rick and I had a few conversations about how we could help, and how much. We were certainly eager and able to look at houses with Matt. The experience of buying a house has changed since Rick and I purchased ours. The economy, housing market, and rules around home financing are significantly different. In and around Seattle, home shopping in Matt's price range meant looking at short sales and bank-owned homes, mostly. Many of these houses had been neglected and vacant for a period of time.

In addition to touring homes with Matt, we wanted to help him financially. Rick told me that if Matt found himself in a situation where he needed a little more money, he wanted to help him out. I said that if Matt knew how much we could help, it would make it easier for him to negotiate financing. This is an example of how Rick prefers to keep information close to the vest—that is, when he isn't shooting from the hip. I prefer to lay it all out there so everyone is working from the same knowledge.

We looked at our finances and decided that we could help by offering a chunk of money. We invited Matt and his girlfriend over for dinner and asked frank questions about his financial situation and where he was in the home-buying process. Throughout dinner and our conversation, I grew more excited about his possibilities for homeownership. Toward the end of the evening, Rick and I shared that we wanted to help financially. We told Matt we could add 50 percent more to his savings.

Matt was so genuinely grateful that I was surprised. This was the same person who, as a kid, complained every summer about our lack of a pool or air conditioning, even though we lived in the mild western Washington climate. We tried to model responsible financial habits, but at the time, it was unclear to us whether he took any of that to heart. As a teenager, he found it important to have the latest and greatest cell phone as soon as it came out. Once a very popular model was selling for $349. Matt had to have it, and did. The next month, his carrier offered that same phone for only $99, almost a quarter of the price that Matt had paid for it. But now that he has moved out without roommates, he searches for bargains. He has told us about the deals he gets from a discount grocery that is a half-hour drive from his house. Somehow, over the years, he had absorbed some of our financial values and developed a deeper understanding of the worth of a dollar. I don't know exactly when Matt learned that it pays to save and live within your means; I'm just glad he did.

After that night, Matt invited us to go house-hunting a few more times. Rick went with him first and visited a couple of houses that needed a lot of work. One had been in a flood; the other still had cars on blocks in front. There were moisture issues, doubts about the durability of the roof, and questions about what might be inside the walls of each home.

Then the five of us—Matt, his girlfriend, his real estate agent, Rick, and I—looked at three more houses. The first was an older, run-down two bedroom priced $25,000 less than Matt's target. The second was also old and had three bedrooms on almost an acre. It was the most promising one Matt had seen yet. The third, built in 2003, had three bedrooms and a small, well-landscaped yard. After some discussion, Matt decided to make an offer on the three-bedroom home with the large lot. We could see that part of the floor needed to be repaired and that the home was missing a refrigerator. Still, it showed potential.

Matt was able to negotiate some on this bank-owned home and began the process of making it his. Since the property was bank-owned, any inspections Matt did would be just for his own knowledge of potential problem areas; he wouldn't be able to negotiate further based on the results. He was going to do an inspection until he found out that it would require the additional costs of de-winterizing the house beforehand and then re-winterizing it afterward. These costs would eat into his savings that he planned to use for the down payment.

Matt thought that his girlfriend's dad and Rick could take a look around and see how structurally sound the house was. Rick didn't feel comfortable with that. He is a finish carpenter and so hasn't built a whole house. He thought Matt should hire an inspector, even if it cost more money. Instead, Matt asked a general contractor friend of his to take a look around. Matt, his friend, and Rick spent several hours one Saturday morning combing over this house. The friend had been building houses for years and saw a lot of things that we had missed. The chimney was failing, and the fireplace was unusable without some modifications. Matt had been hoping to buy an insert and use that fireplace to heat the house. A bathroom had been closed off, and we didn't know why. There were probably plumbing issues that we couldn't see until the house was de-winterized. We had seen that the roof was missing gutters, but we underestimated how much work was needed to reinstall them. And there was an animal infestation.

Matt felt disheartened by these discoveries, but still wanted to move forward. He was already at the top of his price range because of the size of the property. This house had a lot of potential. He knew he didn't have a lot of money to do repairs, but he felt confident in his motivation and ability to work hard. He also knew he would have help from his girlfriend's dad, a tile and flooring expert, and from Rick. With their know-how and Matt's elbow grease, he thought he could take on this project.

The mortgage company insisted on an inspection of the septic system. This was a requirement for the type of loan Matt wanted. Unfortunately, the system didn't pass inspection—it failed miserably. This home was no longer an option for Matt. He was brokenhearted and understandably so. He had already started mentally planning how he would fix this house.

Between the difficulties with the inspection and the issues that his friend found, I had started thinking that maybe this wasn't the right house. To me, those challenges and findings seemed like warning signals that Matt should heed. If he had somehow been able to find financing to buy this house, he would have been completely stretched financially. He was thinking what I do all the time: "Rick can do anything, fix anything, and make anything beautiful." Sadly, there was nothing Rick could have done to fix the septic system. It would have cost thousands of dollars that Matt didn't have.

Matt decided to take a break from house-hunting for a while. During that break, he took a job at Boeing, a major employer in our area. Due to this change in jobs, Matt had to wait quite some time to reapply for a mortgage and look for a house.

Rick and I shared Matt's disappointment that he wasn't able to find the right home. However, we know that he is capable of saving and working toward a large goal. He has seen the difficulties in buying a home. The next time he goes looking for one, he will be even more prepared than he was this time. And though he had to take a step back from being a homeowner, he took several steps forward as a responsible adult.

Sunday brunch

If you have kids, it's important to talk to them about money so they understand the reasons for your financial decisions. When you do this, you share your values and beliefs, especially as they relate to money. Be as forthcoming as you can, given the age of your children.

During your family brunch, discuss the state of the family's financial situation. Write a family mission statement that includes your values about money, such as independence, integrity, honesty, and charity. Also include your financial expectations and responsibilities.

GETTING ORGANIZED

- Make saving a habit. Encourage your children to put a percentage of their allowance and monetary gifts into savings, whether for college or for other goals.

- Raise entrepreneurs. Help your children dream up creative ways to earn their own money, such as by making and selling crafts or by raking a neighbor's leaves.

- Remember that your daily behavior around money—your sensible or irrational purchases, your avoidance of calls from debtors, and so on—can make a powerful impression on your kids. This impression can be just as lasting as the lessons you try to teach them.

- Prepare your young adults to leave the nest. They should be able to carry out the day-to-day duties of a consumer, such as budgeting, saving, using credit wisely, and investing. They should have a savings account for the emergencies that can occur when they are living on their own. They should also start saving at least a small amount for their retirement.

12

TIGHTENING THE BELT

In many ways, the phrase "opposites attract" describes Rick and me as a couple. I am shorter than average, and he is taller than average. He's from the baby boomer generation, and I am a Generation Xer. I am more social, and he prefers alone time or in smaller groups. I think ahead, way ahead, and Rick doesn't. Though he carefully plans out any work or other type of carpentry and building project, he usually doesn't plan in advance for the weekend, vacations, or the rest of our lives. You can ask him on Friday afternoon what he is doing that weekend, and most of the time his response will be "I don't know."

On the other end of the spectrum, I will share my five-year, ten-year, and twenty-year plans with Rick. (He listens, then focuses on step one of each plan.) Since I like to plan ahead, I will buy something months before it's needed. For example, when I find flank steaks on sale, I will stock up, buying several and keeping them in the freezer for a quick, weekday dinner. I also like to buy Christmas presents whenever I see something special for friends and family. I keep all the gift-buying details in a notebook that dates back ten years and includes menus, recipes, grocery lists, and oven schedules.

Rick and I have a lot of differences, but a lot of similarities too. Both of us work hard and consider that when we are spending. We don't like to owe money on cars. We both enjoy an eclectic range of music. We relish time outside, either in the yard, on a bike ride, or in the woods. Having a comfortable home and maintaining it are priorities for both of us. We enjoy being with our families and love to host family get-togethers. For us, an evening at home with a movie and a bowl of popcorn is just as nice as going out.

Even with all these things and more in common, when it comes to money, our differences can crop up and cause tension. Take, for example, Rick's tendency to make last-minute decisions as we go along. One year, we were invited to go skydiving with my brother Loren for his birthday. At some point in his past, Rick had decided that if given the opportunity, he would try skydiving. So we agreed to spend a Saturday afternoon in September at an airfield near the Canadian border. As my brother's birthday approached, Rick decided finally to write his will. When he told me this, I was surprised that it wasn't already done. After all, Matt was thirteen years old by then. I thought Rick was very responsible, so I was stunned that making a will hadn't been a priority. Obviously, Matt's mom would have taken care of him if something had happened to Rick, but what if she hadn't been around to do so? Who then would have cared for Matt until he reached legal age? And what about the financial side of the picture? Matt would have inherited everything Rick left him, but how was he supposed to have managed those assets? Who would have administered the money for Matt as Rick would have wished? Rick's ex-wife? One of his sisters? His mom? Without a will to designate these responsibilities, the state would have decided for him. Thank goodness Rick hadn't been hit by a bus or a falling piano. And even though he finished his will in time, thank goodness his parachute opened, enabling him to land safely after jumping out of the airplane.

CONFLICTS AND COMPROMISES

Figuring out how to make day-to-day decisions as a couple hasn't always been easy. For example, even though we both enjoy making our home more comfortable, I have learned the hard way that Rick has a difficult time spending money on that. When we were newlyweds, I wanted Rick to be involved in deciding how to decorate our new home. I would drag him to stores and ask his opinion on this rug or that bedding. It wasn't that I needed his permission to spend the money, but that I wanted him to be involved in the choices. He eventually told me he really didn't enjoy those outings. He said he had faith in my style and was comfortable with how I accomplished our goals with a reasonable amount of money.

After that, we worked out a new system. We had lived in our new home for a year or two when I decided to update the drapes, which were from the previous owners. Rick told me that the last thing he wanted to do was go shopping for curtains. Really, he didn't even want to know how much they cost. He helped me measure the windows, but I went alone or with friends to shop for what we needed for our living room and family room. I brought home different styles and fabrics to see how they would look. I bought new curtain rods and accessories. After much shopping, trying out, and returning, we ended up with windows that fit our style. A few accessories rounded out the look I was going for, and Rick was happy with the outcome.

This worked for us because Rick understood that the accessories were important to finishing the look and spoke up that he did not want to be very involved. We had a general idea of how much we could spend. I put these purchases on our credit card so my buying and returning of materials and accessories wouldn't interrupt our cash flow. After the decorating project was complete, we paid off the credit card, and it was done. This system also worked because the longer we are married and the older I get, the more assertive I am with my opinions. I genuinely felt that it was time to complete this project. I believed that we had the funds available and felt comfortable with the look I had envisioned. After a couple of conversations, Rick had agreed and we were able to proceed from there.

Sometime later, I found myself in the home-improvement store buying light fixtures for the entire downstairs. This was rare: unless I am buying plants for the garden, I don't usually go into home-improvement stores alone. When I came home with my little car full of chandeliers and light covers, I wasn't sure how Rick would react. He was surprised, but happy I had made the purchases. We had talked about replacing the light fixtures, but hadn't made any real progress. I had gotten a great deal on these pieces and even told him how much they cost. He was spared shopping for new light fixtures, making the decisions, and forking over the money. He happily installed these upgrades and removed the builder-grade fixtures. These purchases cemented in his mind that I have good taste and an eye for great deals.

Another hurdle was deciding how to save our money. Though we are both savers at heart, conflicts arose because of how we prefer to save. I like to save a lot and regularly into my retirement accounts. Rick is a union carpenter and will receive a pension when he retires, so saving for retirement isn't a priority for him.

Until he met me, he didn't consider investing into a retirement account. Instead, he preferred having a healthy savings account with three to six months of income set aside in case of an emergency. He was used to occasional lean times between jobs. His savings account kept him above water during these periods. I had a savings account, but I preferred the potential rates of return in my retirement accounts. I had not experienced long gaps between jobs, so a savings account, while important, was not as high of a priority for me. After Rick and I started merging our finances, we compromised by keeping a third of his savings in our savings account, a third in a money market account, and a third invested in a conservative bond portfolio. I still contribute a percentage of my income into my retirement accounts, and now Rick has a retirement account too.

Over the years, I have challenged Rick's choice for our car- and home-insurance provider. I felt uncomfortable dealing with his agent, whom I had never met. This agent had been working with Rick since he first started driving. Every now and then, I would check in with Rick to see if changes were needed so that our coverage was adequate and up to date. He dismissed my concerns because he didn't want to rock the boat or make the call to his agent. I could have called his agent, our agent, but that didn't feel right, either.

Sometimes I would give our information to insurance agents I knew to see if we were insured correctly. A few years ago, one recommended that we stay with our current insurance company because Rick had been involved in an accident. The agent also recommended that we increase our protection amounts on our vehicles and then raise our deductibles to keep the premium in line. I conveyed this information to Rick. He said he would call his agent. He didn't, which further frustrated me.

In 2011, again, I gave our information to an agent I knew and had him do a little research. It turned out that the timing was good for changing insurance companies. We are exactly the kind of homeowners and drivers insurance companies like. We don't make claims often, we pay our premiums on time, and we insure several cars, a home, and additional items. This agent told me that he could save us $800 a year. To me, that seemed like real money, worth the hassle of changing providers. Rick attributed additional value to the fact that he had been a customer of his insurance company for thirty-five years. I agreed that his relationship with the company had value, but questioned if it was worth $800 a year. I felt that there also was value in my relationship with the new prospective agent. Given that relationship, I felt that we would be treated differently from random customers or those who chose their insurance through an Internet service. What's more, the new provider offered additional protection similar to what we would have received if we had been longtime customers, and we would still be saving money.

For a few weeks, we went around and around this subject. Rick didn't see any reason to change. I felt that he was not doing a good job of managing this part of our financial situation. I generally took care of the long-term strategies and our life insurance, so this felt like a natural extension of my responsibilities. But Rick didn't want to give in. In my business, I like to stay in touch with my clients and know what is changing in their lives. I thought his insurance company would too. He told me that he'd received notices and letters from the company asking us to come in and review our policies, but he had never wanted to and so hadn't set up a meeting. I said that was exactly the reason why he shouldn't get the deciding vote on this issue. And other than the fact that he had been with that company for as long as he had, along with his assumption that he would receive good treatment because he was a longtime customer, he didn't have any other good reasons for staying with them.

He finally set up a meeting to discuss the rates with his insurance agent. However, I didn't meet the guy who had been insuring Rick's family for a few decades; I met his son. His dad was distancing himself from the practice as he got closer to retirement and letting his son take over more responsibilities. So that the son could compare apples to apples, we showed him the numbers we had from the agent I had contacted. Even though we had been customers for years, he could not beat those rates.

I scheduled a follow-up meeting with the agent I wanted to work with so Rick could meet him and go over any concerns he had. Rick decided to let go of the issue, and after that we made the switch. Since then, Rick has acknowledged that he doesn't think about our insurance much, just as he didn't before. Now we are saving money with the same or better protection than we had. I handle our reviews with the agent, and Rick doesn't have to meet with an agent unless he wants to.

The hard part for us was having the discussions. It was difficult for Rick to realize that he was holding on so tightly to this issue. It was difficult for me to explain, without screaming and yelling and becoming a nag, why he wasn't doing a good job of managing the insurance. I don't like to raise my voice, cry, and get overemotional, but I will be the first to admit that I do these things—especially when I feel that I am not being heard and understood.

A few years ago, Rick said that he noticed a change in my behavior toward him. He felt that I used to find certain aspects of him cute, but that I had since become irritated by them. I explained that his quirks were still cute, but that I felt comfortable telling him what else I thought about them. Rick has acknowledged that since he is older, he is probably more set in his patterns and more inflexible than I am. The interesting part is that I have also gotten older. I am only two years younger than Rick was when we first started dating. As I have grown older, I have become much more confident than I was in my twenties. I feel very strongly about some things and say so. I don't cave in as much as I once did. This means that we have to work harder to compromise and must renegotiate our roles occasionally.

The hardest times for us are usually when Rick is in between jobs. He calls these periods "time to tighten the belt." As a neighbor puts it, these are days to "hunker down." The conflict occurs when I come home with something new and Rick becomes quiet. This means I have just spent money on something that he doesn't feel is a priority because he has found out that he won't be needed at work for a while. Suddenly, we are in belt-tightening mode, and I've found out too late. Sometimes I have returned a purchase as a result, and sometimes I haven't. It depended on the item and how important it was to me.

Belt-tightening mode can be interesting. Most often, it means that we cook at home more, stretch the time between trips to Costco, and defer large purchases. Sometimes it also means not talking about a big project that needs to be done. For instance, the hand-railing and floorboards on our deck are failing and should be replaced. For several summers, we have put off doing this. It hasn't been a priority we talk about for several reasons. First, we can't agree on what the new deck should look like. Second, we have other less expensive projects much higher on our priority list. Rick's dilemma during belt-tightening mode is that he has the time and skill to tackle a project like the deck, but he is reluctant, when between jobs, to part with the money for the materials.

Conflict also happens when we hunker down for an extended period. During this time, I am still working and, after a while, my belt loosens. However, Rick's doesn't. I go back to having lunch, instead of coffee, with associates. Plans for the future start bubbling up in my head. Meanwhile, he is doing the housecleaning and shopping and cooking dinner. Seeing him at these tasks, I am reminded that he is in belt-tightening mode and that I need to keep a more careful eye on my expenses.

Some days are better than others. While he is good at making dinner, I can sense that his discontent with the situation lies just beneath the surface. The first week of not working, he enjoys sleeping in, tinkering in the garage, and tending to yard work. The second week, he folds laundry, grocery shops, and catches up with old coworkers. Sometime after that is when he starts growing restless. The recession and downturn in commercial building have only aggravated this. The times in between jobs have grown longer, and the duration of a job is shorter than it used to be.

Whenever Rick returns to work, getting used to the new routine takes us a week or two. His alarm goes off early in the morning. I enjoy that early start to the day too. When he isn't working and only my alarm goes off, it is harder to climb out of bed. Rick working means lunchmeat and more fruit in the refrigerator for his lunches. And I have to remember that he isn't going to do all the dishes or fold the laundry anymore. I can cook dinner, or we prepare it together instead.

MAKING ADJUSTMENTS

Your perspective on money can change daily. Similar to Rick and me, some couples have unwritten rules about how much they can spend without consulting each other first. Others agree upon actual rules. Even with such rules, each partner's sense of what is okay to spend can change during a given day or week. As the price of gas has risen, I have become much more sensitive about money on the days when I have to fill my gas tank. And when I came home with a parking ticket one day, Rick was irrationally reluctant to spend money on basic necessities at the grocery store. Your reactions to financial situations will vary, even when you are presented with the same information. You can't expect anything different from your partner. Sometimes you have to adjust to his or her changed perspective.

From 2010 to 2012, Rick and I regularly looked at our priorities and made adjustments based on where we were financially each month. From a technical standpoint, the recession ended in the summer of 2009. Still, the economy has been recovering slowly. Not only has our personal economy changed, but the personal economies of many. The news is full of stories and statistics showing that people today are less likely to use credit and more likely to save money. New vocabulary has entered our everyday conversations: *staycation, bailout, toxic assets,* and *recessionista.* Being able to adjust is now an important aspect of handling finances, whether you are married, single, or somewhere in between.

Over time, changes that Rick and I made to survive a short spell of unemployment have become a standard of how we operate. More often than ever before, we talk about how we spend and save money. Having these conversations more frequently makes them less difficult. I make a concerted effort to be mindful of what Rick is worried about, and he is learning to do the same for me.

Going out for happy hour is one way that we try to be more intentional with our relationship during this period. This gives us a chance for a change of scenery while we talk. For us, this conversation is different from the usual download at the end of the day. It's a time to celebrate what happened during the week and talk about what's next. On Fridays, we find a restaurant, order a couple of glasses of wine, and make a light dinner out of happy hour food specials. Also, we usually don't talk about bills, and we speak of money only in a very broad sense. These outings have become a special time for us to reconnect.

We don't always go out to reconnect. Sometimes we stay home and put together something different from our regular weeknight dinner. If Rick has been making dinner during the week, then I prepare a light meal for us to nibble on. We set up in the living room or on the deck instead of at the kitchen table, often lighting a fire or candles and playing music in the background. These evenings have an indulgent quality without the high price tag of a dinner and a movie, and that adds to their appeal.

This time also helps us collaborate and get on the same page about what's next. Even with our weekly reconnect, we still fight about money occasionally, but it is usually because of when we spend and not because of what we spend it on. We keep moving forward. Our goals for the future have helped us clarify our spending priorities today. The difference is that I usually want to move forward now and have it done. Rick wants to wait until we are more stable financially. The time we've spent talking about dreams, the future, and what's next has drawn us closer together on issues that we might have fought about. It has made it easier for us to compromise and find a middle ground.

FINDING WHAT WORKS

People have made an infinite number of adjustments to the current economic situation. Parents who stay home with their kids, cut coupons, and plan a week's worth of meals are celebrated for their creativity and knack for finding a bargain. Some viewers have eliminated cable TV and are using alternative means to watch movies, shows, and news. Using daily deal websites and group-rate offers is common. The concept of layaway has returned to some retail stores. Libraries are full of people using their resources. Ridership on public transportation has increased. Savings accounts are getting healthier. When making a purchase, shoppers are asking themselves, "Is this worth it?" Finding the balance between saving and spending is difficult. You also must strike a balance between saving for what you need now and saving for the future. But the benefit of doing so, and of making these adjustments, is becoming more mindful of where your dollars go.

I used to wonder when we would ever repair or rebuild the deck. I don't anymore because of how our priorities have clarified. Even throughout this economic downturn, we are working toward our dreams and plans for the future. The deck in its current state is still functional. When we repair it, we will do so with the resale of our house in mind. Any former plans of a large deck that landed on a sweeping flagstone terrace are gone, along with many other old ideas.

This mindfulness of where we spend our dollars is what works for Rick and me. It means being very aware of each other's perspective on our financial situation. It also means questioning old ideas about what people are supposed to do with money and deciding what is appropriate for us. We have renegotiated our roles and responsibilities sometimes to allow for change. We care enough about each other to have a conversation and not make unilateral decisions. That is an important feature in creating a partnership. Ideas of right and wrong, of good habits and bad habits, are superseded by the question of whether a purchase or investment is in line with our priorities.

Sunday brunch

....

- Where do your priorities line up with your partner's? Where do compromises need to be made?

- When you two are struggling, what do you do to "fight fair"?

- What behaviors do you avoid?

- Do gender assumptions, old labels, or roles interfere with your working together as a team?

- Are your short-term and long-term goals spelled out clearly for both of you to see and work toward?

13

A CABIN IN THE WOODS

Dreams are fascinating. I have so many of them. Some can be categorized into a bucket list, some are impossible, and some I am making happen right now. I talk to people about their dreams all the time. What dreams can they fulfill now? What dreams will wait until after they've achieved financial independence? What dreams do they want to help their children accomplish?

An aspiration of mine is to have a large vegetable garden that would feed us all year. I would love to have the time to do that much cultivating. Finding ways to preserve and store the harvest and having a cellar full of jars and root vegetables has a certain appeal. My far-out dreams include being able to time travel and being a man for a day, just to see what those experiences would be like.

Rick has dreamed about going into outer space. He loves movies and history specials about the space program, the space race, and astronauts. Fortunately for Rick, others with greater resources than we have are working to help people like him make that dream a reality.

I would love to travel to all the countries where we spent time when I was younger, when my dad was in the Navy. My memories of those places are tied to the things that were important to me at my age when we lived there. One memory from Italy is sitting on my dad's shoulders when we saw a man wearing a white robe in a window, waving at us while we stood in St. Peter's Square. If I had been older, I would have recognized him as Pope John Paul II. I probably also would have made time for shoe shopping. When we lived in Okinawa, Japan, there was a tree house in the botanical gardens by our home that we would sneak into and drink sodas while we watched people go by. In my mind, the tree house was way up in the tree, where people walking by couldn't see us. I wonder how it would appear now.

DARING TO DREAM

Rick is far more pragmatic than I. For him, dreams seem so nebulous that he barely has the courage to say them out loud. During our first year together, we took a weekend trip to Leavenworth, Washington. We stayed at a cute bed-and-breakfast in the country and went exploring during the day. While driving around the countryside, we saw a friendly log cabin by the river. Bikes and kayaks were leaning against its walls. We could smell the barbecue going and hear laughter. After we drove by, Rick said, "That would be nice." I was intrigued by this idea and opened a conversation about what was so nice.

There are so many wonderful places to visit, and many of them would be nice places to live. One example is a house on the beach where you could watch the waves. You could walk the beach every day and pick up pieces of glass made smooth by the sea and sand. Alternatively, a flat in the city could offer endless possibilities of dining and entertainment, all within blocks. Some might prefer a boat, with room to sleep, where they could decide at a moment's notice to head down the coast or across the ocean. At one point, Rick and I toyed with the idea of writing to the owners of the farm his grandparents once owned. It spans twenty-four acres, including beachfront in Waldport, Oregon, three hours south of Cannon Beach, Oregon. In that letter, we would have let them know that if they ever wanted to sell, they should contact us because we might be interested in buying it. Even with these other interests, Rick's happy place has long been a cabin in the woods where he can sit by the fire, hear the stream gurgling, and watch the stars twinkle brighter as the sun sets.

I learned that a log cabin surrounded by trees in the woods was something that he had thought about occasionally, especially when he went camping. My active imagination immediately went to work designing this cabin with vaulted ceilings, cozy places to snuggle and read, and a wine cellar. Rick's requirements were much simpler. He wanted a bedroom in a loft and trees all around—lots of trees.

He is a little peculiar about trees. A few years ago, new neighbors cleared a dozen or so trees from their yard. I could tell that this irritated him. As he was telling me, his eyes were intent and angry. The next day, he went out to our yard and found Douglas fir saplings that had taken root, like weeds, in various places. He planted those saplings in a bare flower bed along a fence. "There. I think I planted one for every one they cut down," he proudly stated. Rick would never describe himself as a tree hugger. But there he was, loving on those baby trees.

I found the notion of a log cabin in the woods very charming and promptly started doing a little research and putting together ideas for when it might be possible for this to happen. Whenever we traveled or went camping, I carried a small notebook with me. In this notebook, I captured ideas and thoughts about what properties the land would have. Trees, mountains, and wide-open spaces were definitely on the list. Water nearby would be nice. Ideally, the property would be no farther than a two-hour drive from our home. Soon, the notebook was full of driveway drawings, house designs, cutaways, and lists.

Inevitably, when we were sitting around a fire, talking and thinking about all the possibilities for the cabin, I would have a moment of determination, pull out my notebook, and start writing down dates. Working backward from Rick's retirement date, I would calculate how long it would take us to locate a property, figure out what we wanted, and then build it. The funny thing is, I can look back at that notebook and find several entries with deadlines for buying the property. Most are already in the past. Even back then, I was feeling the pressure that we were behind schedule for manifesting this dream.

Sometimes we would have difficulty talking about this dream. Rick felt that it would never happen because we would never have enough money and he would never feel secure enough. And, he supposed, all the best places were already taken. I was frustrated that I had to keep selling him on the possibility. After yet another discussion, he would reconfirm that this was something he wanted, and then we would try to move forward.

Now, our financial independence plans revolve around moving to the sunnier side of the mountains. Eastern Washington holds a lot of appeal for us. Besides having more sunshine, that area has wineries, orchards, and more mountains and valleys for us to explore. It also offers a slower pace, which we are looking forward to adopting. Thinking about living more simply and closer to the land makes me feel as if I have just let out a big sigh.

Rick is eligible for early retirement from his union in a few years. He would like the opportunity to explore another career or be in business for himself. The possibilities range from learning a new trade or starting a brewery to becoming a photographer or planting a Christmas tree farm. We still have a few years to figure it out.

In 2009, I felt that it was the year the cabin would finally happen. The year before, we had put our financing in order to buy property if we found something during our travels. My car payments ended in 2009, and in Rick's mind, the payment on a new piece of property would simply replace them. The real estate market was in a difficult situation, which we thought could work in our favor.

Previously, in 2005, we had set aside a chunk of money from the sale of my condo. At that time, I hoped that we could use those funds on a property where we could build. Rick was worried that my ten-year-old car was approaching that time in its life when it would need more maintenance. He wanted to use some of that money as a down payment on a car. I thought my car was fine, and I was willing to sacrifice having a newer car if that would bring us one step closer to our dream. I also felt that since the money came from real estate, it was fitting that it should go back into real estate. However, Rick apparently wasn't comfortable yet with the idea of owning more land, so I bought a new car.

Four years later, in the spring of 2009, we went over the mountains looking for property for the first time with a real estate agent. We laid out our requirements: five acres or more, trees, a view, and sunshine. Initially, we thought that we would end up near an area where Rick went camping often when he was younger. But all the properties we looked at in that area were too expensive, too shady, too open, or lacking in trees or accessibility. In other words, they weren't right. I fell in love with one in particular, but Rick wasn't happy with the slope of the driveway and the lack of trees. We crossed the mountains one more time that spring to look at property, but we did not find what we were seeking.

That summer was especially busy. We finally headed east again in October to look in different areas with a new real estate agent. We went farther north and east, almost three hours from home. This area offered wider views and better affordability, although it was farther away. Rick fell in love with one of the first properties we visited. It turned out to be everything he wanted: It was in the mountains, about two thousand feet in elevation. There were a lot of trees on the property and in the surrounding areas. A stream, First Creek, ran through the lot, and it offered a great view of Lake Chelan. Rick liked that the property wasn't too far from town. In his head, he heard a little voice say, "This could work."

I wasn't so sure about that property. I was thinking about driving late at night, when the pavement would be icy, up the narrow, winding road that led to it. I was also concerned about the neighbors, their barking dogs, and the possible disputes about property lines and easements. Our real estate agent had told us about an email that he received from a neighbor of this property who was selling his lot. The neighbor was contesting where an easement lay that offered access to the property we were touring.

We spent the rest of the weekend viewing more properties with our agent. He showed us some fantastic views of rivers, mountains, and wide-open spaces. The possibilities in my head jumped higher and faster, from one to the other. I was glad that I wore a seatbelt while we were in the truck to keep me from floating out of my seat. With some of these properties, it was difficult to see certain details, so at the end of the evening we created a list of questions about each property to ask our agent.

Over two and a half days, we returned to that property on First Creek three more times. The view of the lake was incredible. We met a couple of the neighbors and learned a little of their story. They were not as scary as I had imagined them. Sometimes when you are buying property that far off the grid, you don't know what kind of neighbors you will get. But these neighbors were so friendly. They had just built a home that year. They had owned their property for fifteen years and enjoyed it as a getaway. This would be their first winter in the mountains. The wife told me that she had been praying for neighbors. Later, we happened to run into the other neighbors, who were selling their lot and who had issues with the easement location. Even though they were questioning that detail, the husband and wife were still nice and shared the history of the property with us.

The situation involved an interesting reversal for Rick and me. He is usually the skeptic, and I am the one encouraging us to move forward. He was sure that this was the property where we would build our future home. He was surprised that land with acreage as nice as this wasn't already taken and developed. And he was thrilled that a lot with a view of the lake was within our price range and fit most of our requirements. I wasn't as sure. With mountains on both sides, it felt almost claustrophobic instead of cozy. There were so many trees that I was afraid we would have to cut down a lot of them. This property did not lend itself to becoming a Christmas tree farm. Also, I wanted the easement issue put to rest.

I was looking for affirmations that this property was the right choice. After all, it was a big decision for us. We had been looking forward to and planning for this moment a long time. I was also surprised at how easily we had found this property. Maybe if we kept looking, we would find something even more amazing,

I thought. But on our last walk around the property, I had my confirmation. While Rick was tromping through the underbrush, studying the property borders, I smelled a fresh, green scent on the breeze. I remembered this smell. It is my oldest memory. I think it is the smell outside the home where I was born, although I am not sure—we moved from there when I was three years old. It reminds me of feeling safe and feeling at home. After remembering that scent, I was able to advance another step in my mind. I let go of some of my doubt, enabling us to move forward together on this project. I started trusting in Rick's assuredness and my ability to make anything work. If he was ready and this was it, then I could accept that this property offered most of what we wanted.

We made a lowball offer and were surprised that it was accepted right away. The seller was very motivated and asked only how quickly we could close on the deal. While we waited to close, we further investigated the easement issue until we were satisfied. Within weeks, we were the proud owners of eight acres of mountainside, trees, a creek, and a lake view. That winter, we watched the weather over the pass and on the east side of the mountains with more interest. We had to wait for spring to start building. I longed for a camera system that overlooked our property so we could see how much snow had accumulated and watch the wildlife around the new homestead.

We took a trip with Matt that winter to show him the property. In his four-wheel drive truck, we were easily able to navigate the winter roads. An energetic snow fight started as soon as we arrived. We saw an eagle fly slowly overhead. We chatted about different sites where we could build a cabin during the summer and a house in a few years.

The hardest part at that point was waiting. We had to wait for the ground to be in a condition suitable to test for a septic system. We also had to wait to drill a well. And until the ground was hard enough to support heavy equipment, we couldn't establish a driveway. Rick received a new chainsaw for his birthday and was eager to get over to this land and start using it to clean up trees that had fallen.

One day that winter, I watched a TV show about a couple who were selling their home in the States to buy a house in Cabo San Lucas, Mexico. I watched only for a few minutes, but it was long enough for me to think that we would never get to do that. Never mind that Rick would probably never move to another country. All of a sudden, the realization that we owned this property felt as if it were tying me down. This feeling was probably not unlike the realization I had when I bought my first home. Still, it surprised me.

When I shared this reaction with Rick, he was speechless at first. Then he said he didn't know what to do with that information. He had never considered the possibility that I would feel this way. I was scared that I was stuck, and now I had scared him that I didn't really want this land. Fortunately, it didn't take me very long to overcome my fear. We don't need to buy a house in Mexico or another exotic locale to be happy. We can always travel to those locations and know that we have accomplished one of our dreams.

I tease Rick that he would never have been able to make this dream come true without me. Honestly, my dreams never could have come true without him. It was through our adventures and conversations that this dream started becoming a reality. The clearer your vision is, the easier it is to make progress toward that dream. And the stronger your dream is, the more easily you can defer immediate gratification and save for the future.

I have friends who recently sold everything for a multiyear trip around the world. Their trip didn't happen all of a sudden; they planned it for years. Once they decided it was something they wanted to do, they got busy researching, planning, and talking to others who had been successful with the same dream. Over time, my friends changed their spending habits and budget so they could save more for their trip. They set a date for their departure and sold most of their belongings. We are the happy recipients of the contents of their kitchen. Those items will be perfect for setting up our kitchen in the cabin. They are blogging about their adventures so others can make their dreams a reality too.

We are still taking steps toward our big dream. We spent weekends throughout the summer of 2010 building the shell of a two-hundred-square-foot cabin that would act as temporary housing while we figure out what we will do with the rest of the property. During the construction of the cabin, we had numerous conversations about money and priorities. Rick grew frustrated with my timelines, and I became irritated when he hadn't planned ahead. Still, all that effort couldn't take away from the peaceful feeling I get in the morning when we are there. That hour before Rick wakes up and I can sit outside with a book and a cup of coffee is one of my favorite times. At our house, it is usually too cold or wet to sit outside in the morning. During that hour, while I watch the sun come up, I am most sure that this is the right place for us. Plus, at our house, we don't have the view we do from the cabin.

THE FIVE-YEAR PLAN

In the end, we would like a larger cabin where our whole family could come for a week for Thanksgiving. This would include flexible sleeping quarters, a large kitchen, and a great room. Other requirements are a stone fireplace, an outdoor living space, and a spacious shop where Rick can tinker on larger projects. Ideally, it would feel like Christmas and Sunday morning all the time on this property. Nieces, nephews, and our god-kids could spend weeks there in the summer. They could explore the woods, cool off in the lake, and make s'mores in the evening.

It took a lot of preparation for us finally to reach this stage, even though we are far from done. We consulted mortgage lenders, financial advisors, and accountants to see how this would affect our current financial situation. We talked about our vision often and took notes about what was important to us. Even when we were on vacation in an exotic locale, nowhere near the woods, we would think about what it was that we were trying to build. On vacation, it was sometimes easier to dream and discuss those priorities. Since we were detached from the routines of our daily lives, we could detach further from our limitations and dream even bigger or move the dream forward.

Dreams are powerful. They carry us through difficult situations. They inspire us and help us move forward. They elevate our thinking above the daily details that can weigh us down. They help us find balance between saving and spending now, and saving and spending in the future.

When thinking about your dreams, it is sometimes helpful to write them down, mind map, or journal about them. If you are more creative, try drawing or painting to focus those dreams further. Say your dreams out loud to people who will support you. Sometimes the people you think will support you won't. In that case, find other people to listen to your dreams who will be supportive.

Ask about your partner's dreams. Are they similar to yours? Are these dreams something that you two can work toward together? Talk about what resources you have that would strengthen the dreams. What small steps can you do today that will propel the dreams forward? Someone once said that goals that are not written down are just wishes. Whether it is a goal, a wish, or a dream, some idea is moving you forward. With a goal, as compared to a dream, you can get too attached to the outcome.

With goals, you create steps, deadlines, and measurements of success. I did that when I set deadlines for when we needed to buy our property. That put pressure on me to get Rick moving. When I wasn't able to do that, I felt that we were running behind. With a dream, sometimes it is helpful to let go and see what happens. While reaching for a dream, you can still talk about it, journal about it, and work toward it. The difference is in the deadlines and attachment to exactly how and when the dream will become reality.

One dream can even launch you into the next dream. That is an incredible experience. In the area where we bought our property, there is a lot of farmland. My dream of growing a large vegetable garden that could sustain us is also a little closer to realization as a result. Before that happens, we will need to finish our little cabin, locate the site for our house, build that house, and move there permanently. Still, every step toward one dream brings me closer to the other.

Know that dreams also shift and change. As you grow older, as life takes you down a different path, your dreams may become different than they once were. Even so, keep dreaming. Keep saying those dreams out loud. Keep taking small steps toward your dreams.

Sunday brunch

- What are your dreams? Your partner's dreams?

- Who can help you move forward with these dreams?

- What else do you need to have in place to bring your dreams closer to reality?

CONCLUSION

Rick and I took the vacation of a lifetime last Christmas, in 2011. Our destination: China. My brother Loren and sister-in-law Sarah had just moved to Shanghai. Both are teachers with two-year contracts at an international school. Loren teaches humanities, and Sarah teaches art. Earlier last year, we made up our mind to go to China and spend Christmas with them. My youngest brother, Ryan, and his partner said they would join us on the trip. The plan was to save over the course of the year so we could enjoy our trip guilt-free.

Unfortunately, it was a tough year. Rick and I didn't earn what we had in the past. In August, Ryan bought tickets, but we still hadn't committed 100 percent. I was determined to go on this trip and went to work persuading Rick. He had committed earlier in the year, when December seemed a long way off. Rick doesn't go on vacation easily. He prefers to go when he is between jobs, but it is hard to plan for that. Also, money can be tight during those times. He doesn't like to take vacations when he is on a job because he hates to miss the work. But since he usually works in commercial and retail buildings, the chances were good that he wouldn't be working when we wanted to make our trip.

His hesitation wasn't just about the money. Other barriers were the food, language, and hassle of flying across the world. Rick can be a picky eater. He doesn't like chicken or seafood. He tends to cook the same things repeatedly, as he does on Taco

Tuesdays. I reminded him that we would mostly be eating with Loren and Sarah. We could cook at their apartment most of the time. Sarah is a vegetarian, so he could always eat what she ate.

At some point, Rick gave in and helped me do what was needed to go on this trip. He realized that we were fortunate to have family to stay with and show us around. All of that would help reduce the cost of the trip. Because Loren and Sarah would be our tour guides, we didn't spend much time learning the language or culture beforehand. Flying across the world would be a bit of a barrier, though. And to enter China, we had to get visas. For Americans, the cost is three times as much as it is for anyone else. We planned to be there for a couple of weeks around Christmas and New Year's Day. Since we were going during the holidays, the tickets cost more than usual. Also, because we would be gone at Christmas, I planned to buy Christmas presents for everyone on our list while we were there. I joked that we were reducing costs by cutting out the middleman and buying our presents direct from where they were made.

We had managed to save some money for daily expenses, and we put the visas and the airline tickets on a credit card. We left a few days before Christmas, packed for the cold weather in Beijing and the milder weather of Shanghai. Overall, the trip was amazing. Loren and Sarah were great hosts. They showed us all their favorite local places. Spending time in their apartment meant that we got to hang out and weren't on the go all the time. We saw the Great Wall of China and the Forbidden City. We spent time at several local markets shopping for faux antiques and Christmas presents. The gardens and temples that we saw were beautiful, even in winter. And though we came home with credit card debt, we were both glad we went. Neither of us has any regrets about that trip.

The China trip has prompted even more conversations about our dreams. As I write this, I am sitting at the picnic table outside of our cabin, looking at Lake Chelan. We come here often, and being away from the pressure and stresses of work and home life gives us the opportunity to expand on plans for our future. Those plans always involve conversations about money.

We are still making progress on our land and cabin. Rick is now building the kitchen, which will replace the plywood counter and sawhorses where I currently cook. We are consulting with an architect on the building of our future home here.

Matt has achieved one of his dreams as well. In the spring of this year, he purchased his first home. He has all the exuberance and energy of a young person whipping a fixer-upper into shape. When he comes home from work, he builds shelves in the garage, replaces worn-out fixtures, or paints. In his new house, he has room for a band to practice. I hope that he achieves the dream of becoming a professional musician, too.

This year, 2012, we took another trip to China to visit Loren, Sarah, and my new niece, Jade. On that trip, we did a little sightseeing, but spent most of our time smiling at this perfect baby and trying to get her to smile back at us. Sarah and Loren continue to live their dreams of travel and adventure, now with a baby in a backpack.

During the trip, we decided to visit Scotland and England in 2013. Rick's heritage is English and Scottish, and mine is Welsh on my father's side. This journey has been a dream of Rick's, and if we can go to China twice, then England and Scotland should be a piece of cake. Someday, I also want to take him back to the Philippines to visit all my aunts, uncles, and cousins. It is another beautiful country that I haven't been to in over twenty years.

Another dream of mine has been to share this story. Getting

this book published has been a long journey. At times it was frustrating and heartbreaking, then joyful and inspired. It's amazing that my computer didn't short out from all my crying episodes while I was writing. In the end, the book has been worth every joyful or frustrated tear. True, I don't have all the answers to the money issues couples face. But I hope that by sharing what is in my heart, I will inspire you to share what is in yours. Then you and your partner can build from there.

ACKNOWLEDGMENTS

W riting this book has been a labor of love. It began on a Sunday morning after I watched *The Notebook*. I wanted to document our love story, just as the film's protagonist, Allie, documented hers. I wrote a few pages and then they sat. Later, I met Zita Gustin, who encouraged me to keep writing and to meet and talk to other women writers. She introduced me to Jan B. King, who worked with me on how to tell a great story that would resonate with readers. Debbie Whitlock and the rest of the Seattle-Bellevue chapter of the eWomenNetwork have encouraged me all along the way. They are my champions and loudspeakers. I appreciate all of them.

Brook Taylor is the most amazing editor. She has a warm approach and provides input in a gentle way. Working with her gave me even more courage to share this story. Lori Zue and Elizabeth Rightor helped shape the quality and intention of this book from its inception. Big thanks to Jeni Dahn for encouraging me to share my truth. Karen Lynn Maher of Legacy One Authors made sure that all the details were tended to before the book went to print. I am also grateful to Annette Grupido, a fantastic real estate agent who helped us find *our* home.

My warm thanks to the women of Quantum Leap—Leona, Laurie, Lorina, Laura, and Caroline—who have sustained, inspired, and pushed me. Lori Hazlett made me look good even when I was not around. Leann Groby and Karla Stevens rescued me with a bottle of wine and a chicken salad every time I was in need. I also want to thank the people I encounter every day who have inspired and motivated me.

I shared this book with my brothers, Loren and Ryan, to discover any inaccuracies in my account of our family history. They provided just the right feedback. Ryan, my baby brother, read the book in a day and enthusiastically expressed how much he loved it. Loren, the English teacher, read it throughout a month and responded with plenty of queries and corrections. Both reactions were full of love and acknowledgment for my mission.

Sarah is the sister I've always wanted. The time we've spent together, though limited, has meant the world to me. For her affirmation that my work helps couples make sense of money, I am grateful. I also thank Ryan Ceurvorst, whom I call for last-minute tech support and a great sounding board.

I am so lucky to have amazing parents, Dennis and Amy Digges. I thank my dad for including me in financial conversations that were way over my head, starting when I was very young. I thank my mom for always telling me that I could do anything I wanted to do.

I thank Matt for being who he is and for providing hours of discussion and pages of content. I am so proud of him and love him very much. And finally, to my husband, Rick, I am grateful for the love, support, and encouragement that are the reasons I keep reaching for our dreams.

GLOSSARY

Income The amount of money that you earn over a period of time. Income is money that comes into your life.

Expense The amount of money that you spend over a period of time. Expense is money that goes out of your life.

Balance sheet A statement showing how much you own and owe at a specific point in time.

Assets Valuable items you own at a specific point in time.

Liabilities Debts and obligations that you owe at a specific point in time.

Net worth or equity The value of what you own minus what you owe: assets - liabilities = net worth or equity.

Financial statements The set of statements that describe your financial situation, including your income statement and balance sheet.

Creditors People, businesses, or other organizations to which you owe money.

Loan Money borrowed and repaid under agreed-upon terms and conditions.

Credit score A number roughly between three hundred and eight hundred that measures an individual's credit worthiness and indicates to lenders that person's capacity to repay his or her debts. This score can be a very big factor in determining whether you will get a loan and from whom, as well as what interest rate and fees you will be charged for your loan.

Staycation A vacation spent at home or nearby.

Recessionista A woman who remains stylish on a tight budget.

Toxic asset An asset that is worth a lot more than its listed value on a balance sheet. Its value may be so uncertain that there is no market for the asset, and the owner may not be able to recover the value.

Bailout A rescue from financial distress.

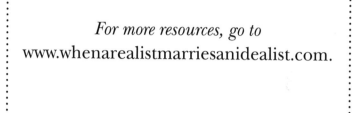

For more resources, go to
www.whenarealistmarriesanidealist.com.

ABOUT THE AUTHOR

Stacy Willoughby has worked in the financial services industry since 2001 and remains a hopeless romantic. She is passionate about helping couples, especially newlyweds, start off on the right foot financially. A Seattle native, she lives in Bothell, Washington, with her husband, Rick, and his cat, Sophie.